The child in the family

Maria Montessori is regarded as one of the most brilliant and
original thinkers of the nineteenth and twentieth centuries.
An Italian educator and Doctor of Medicine, she worked in
the fields of psychiatry, hygiene, pedagogy and anthropology.
She revolutionized modern educational thought by stressing
freedom of expression, self-education and sense training.
Based upon her innovative methods, she founded several
schools throughout Europe and India as well as an educational
institute for mentally defective children. Included among her
works on education are *The Discovery of the Child* and *The
Absorbent Mind*. Maria Montessori was the mother of four
children. She died in 1952 at the age of eighty-two.

Also available in this series

Child development series

Maria Montessori

The child in the family

Translated by Nancy Rockmore Cirillo

Pan Books Ltd London and Sydney

First published in Great Britain 1975 by
Pan Books Ltd, Cavaye Place, London SW10 9PG
ISBN 0 330 24401 9
© 1956 and translation © 1970
by
Maria Montessori, heir of Dr. Mario Montessori
First published in Italy as *Il bambino in famiglia* by Garzanti Editore

Printed in Great Britain by
Richard Clay (The Chaucer Press) Ltd, Bungay, Suffolk

CONTENTS

1
THE
BLANK
PAGE

Our method—which bears my name in order to distinguish it from other modern attempts to create new educational forms—has led to the discovery of previously unobserved moral characteristics in children. Indeed, what emerged before us was the figure of a child yet to be discovered.

And it was because of our discoveries, and to further the understanding of children and to work for their defense and the recognition of their rights, that we were impelled to direct social action. Moreover, we were impelled to act because children are weak human beings who live among the strong; they are not understood, and their profound needs are unrecognized by adult society. Such a fact represents an abyss of unsuspected evils.

Children in our schools, which are places where they can work quietly, where their repressed spirits can expand and reveal themselves, demonstrated attitudes and modes of action remote from popular notions about childhood, and we were thus forced to reflect upon the gravity of the serious educational errors committed in the past, always upon the most delicate members of the human race.

Our children revealed to us a level of mind yet unexplored, and their activities manifested tendencies never dealt with by psychologists or educators. For instance, the children were never attracted to objects, such as toys, which were supposed to please them, nor were they interested in fairy tales. Instead, they all sought to free themselves from adults and to do everything by themselves, manifesting clearly the desire not to be helped unless such help was absolutely necessary. They were tranquil, absorbed and intensely interested in their work, achieving an amazing level of serenity.

Evidently, our students' natural spontaneity, which derives mysteriously from the child's inner life, had long been suppressed by the energetic and inopportune intervention of adults, who believe they can do everything better than children, substituting their own activities for those of the children and forcing them to submit their will and initiative to adult control.

We adults, in our interpretation and treatment of children, not only have erred in certain details of education, or in some imperfect forms of schooling, but have pursued a course of action which is wholly wrong. And our mistakes have now generated a new social and moral question. The dissension between children and adults has existed unchanged for centuries, but the young have now tipped the balance. It is this reversal that has impelled us to action, not only in the direction of educators, but toward all adults, especially parents.

The wide diffusion of our method has generated schools in every country and among people widely diverse in custom and culture. This testifies to the universality of the dissension between child and adult that oppresses the human being from the moment of his birth and is all the more dangerous in that it is unconscious. In presumably superior civilizations, such as our own, this dissension is exacerbated by the complexity of social custom and by the consequent separation of the child from the natural self and its freedom of action.

The child who lives in an environment

created by adults lives in a world ill-adapted to
his own needs, both physical and, even more
important, psychic (the fulfillment of the latter
needs enables him to develop intellectually and
morally). The child is repressed by a more powerful adult who undercuts his will and constrains
him to adapt to a hostile environment on the
naive assumption that by doing so he is developing the child socially. Almost all so-called
educational activity is pervaded by the notion of
direct—and therefore violent—adaptation by the
child to the adult world. *This adaptation is based
upon an unquestioning obedience, which leads to
the negation of the child's personality, a negation
in which the child becomes the object of a justice
that is no justice, of injury and punishment that
no adult would tolerate.*

This adult attitude is so deeply rooted in the
family that it is applied even to the child who is
greatly loved. Furthermore, it is intensified in the
school, which almost always methodically enforces
direct and premature adaptation to the necessities of the adult environment. In the school, in
fact, rigid classwork and enforced discipline pro-
ject the delicate world of childhood into a perni-
cious and alien atmosphere. Often the accord
between the family and the school resolves itself
into an alliance of the strong against the weak,
whose timid and uncertain voices never seem to

find an audience. The child who seeks to be heard and is wounded by rejection often withdraws in a far more dangerous fashion than mere submission.

A more just and charitable approach toward the child would be to create an "adaptive" environment different from the repressive one in which he operates and which has already formed his character. The implementation of any educational system ought to begin with the creation of an environment that protects the child from the difficult and dangerous obstacles that threaten him in the adult world. The shelter in the storm, the oasis in the desert, the place of spiritual rest ought to be created in the world precisely to assure the healthy development of the child.

No social problem is as universal as the oppression of the child. Historically, the oppressed—slaves, the servant class and finally the workers—were minority groups who sought their redemption through social change, often in open battle between the oppressed and their oppressors. The American Civil War was fought against the institution of slavery, the French Revolution against the ruling classes and modern revolutions to realize new economic forms. These are all examples of the formidable conflicts among groups of adults compelled to resort to violence to right their wrongs.

But the social problem of the child is not one of class, race or nation. The child who does not function socially is one who functions solely as an appendage of the adult. Those who oppress one part of humanity to the advantage of another succeed only in destroying social unity; to see this from the collective point of view, we need only glance down to see that among the suffering and oppressed there are also children. Almost all who care about children point out that it is the child who is the innocent victim of the wrongs that oppress the adult human being. That appendage to the adult, weak and unable to speak for himself, strikes directly to the heart and evokes a special note of compassion and a particular need for charity. There has been much talk of miserable children and happy children, of the poor and the rich, of those who are abandoned and those who are loved. But such talk merely establishes the fact that the contrasts we see among adults are reflected and, indeed, formed in childhood and youth.

What is the child? He is a reproduction of the adult who possesses him as if he were a piece of property. No slave was ever so much the property of his master as the child is of the parent. No servant has ever had the limitless obedience of a child required of him. Never were the rights of man so disregarded as in the case of *the child.* No worker has ever blindly had to follow orders as must the child. At least the worker has his hours off and a place to go for compassionate response. No one has ever had to work like the child, who must submit to an adult who imposes hours of work and hours of play according to a rigid and arbitrary set of rules.

The child as a separate being has never existed socially. It has, therefore, always been desirable that children live in a house comfortable for adults, in which the mother cooks, the father works and the parents care for the children according to their abilities. Schools traditionally respect the family structure as far as possible. This was always considered the best arrangement that could be made for children.

The idea that the child is a personality separate from the adult never seemed to occur to anybody. Almost all moral and philosophical thought has been oriented toward the adult, and social questions about childhood itself have never been asked. The child as a separate entity, with different needs to satisfy in order to attain the highest ends of life, has never been taken into consideration. He is seen as a weak being supported by adults, never as a human being without rights oppressed by adults. The child as a human being who works, as a victim who suffers, as the best of companions, is still an unknown figure. This is the figure about whom there exists a blank page in the history of mankind.

It is this blank page that we would like to fill.

2
THE
NEWBORN
CHILD

We understand civilization as a means by which man may gradually adapt to his environment. If this is so, who experiences a more sudden and radical change in environment than the newborn child? Furthermore, what provision does our civilization make for the newborn child, for this being who, in the birth process, must undergo an adaptation worse than sudden, who literally passes from one existence to another?

There ought to be a page that precedes all the others in the history of civilized man. It should record what he has done to help the newborn child adapt himself to an alien environment. But there is none. The first page of the book of life has yet to be written because no one has attempted to discover the exigencies of new life.

Yet experience has revealed a terrible truth to us: we carry the wrongs of early infancy with us for the rest of our lives. The life of the embryo and the vicissitudes of childhood are decisive—and surely this is universally recognized—for the health of the adult and the future of the race. How is it possible that birth, that most difficult moment in man's entire life, has never been recognized as a crisis not only for the mother but for the child?

The crisis of the newborn lies in his total separation from a mother who, until then, has done everything for him. Separated from her and left to his own inadequate powers, he must instantly rely upon his own vital functions. Until this moment, he grew gently in a warm fluid created especially for him, protecting him from any imbalance or any drop in temperature, the least glimmer of light or the slightest sound.

Yet at birth he is ejected from this home to live in the air. Without the least transition, he is pushed from perfect repose to the exhausting work of being born. His body is crushed almost as if he had passed between two millstones, and he comes to us wounded, like a pilgrim who has journeyed from a distant land. But what do we do to receive him and help him? All attention is turned toward the mother, and the doctor gives the child a cursory examination merely to establish that he is alive and well. The parents contemplate him with profound joy, their egos being well satisfied by this beautiful child who realizes their fondest hope: the adult has a child, and his presence unites the family in feelings of love.

But while the mother rests easily in a darkened room, who thinks to let the child, who is equally tired, rest quietly in a darkened room so that he can adapt himself little by little to his new environment? No one sees in the newborn child the human being who suffers. No one appreciates the sensitivity of a little body that has never before been handled, or of his reactions to innumerable physical impressions and to every unfamiliar touch.

They say that nature provides for its own and gives support when it is necessary. For the rest, every living being must overcome the same trials. But if civilization has created in man a "second nature," one that overrides the natural man and inhibits its free expression, then it might be interesting to see what happens among other animals. If we observe animals, we see that the female hides her young, keeps them from the light for a certain period of time and protects them with the warmth of her body. She guards them jealously and never permits other animals to come near or allows her young to be moved or even looked at.

Yet for the newborn human being, neither nature nor civilization makes any provision to alleviate the difficulty of adaptation. Some say that if the child survives it is enough; their only criterion for judging successful adaptation is that the child has not lost the power to live. The newborn child should be allowed to remain in fetal position after birth, yet he is immediately dressed, and, indeed, at one time he was swaddled, his fragile limbs restrained by force.

It used to be said that the healthy child would resist and adapt, for doesn't all of nature? Why, then, do we try to keep warm in the winter, and have soft blankets and comfortable chairs for easy and congenial living? Are we not stronger than the newborn child? Why don't we live free in the woods if we are so strong?

Death, like birth, is a law of nature, and one to which we must all submit. Why do we seek to ease that terrible moment of death in every possible way? Why, knowing that we cannot conquer death, do we at least want to render it less painful? Yet we never think to alleviate the suffering of birth.

There is in us, finally, a peculiar emptiness, a blindness we have built into our spirit and our civilization. Something like the blind spot in the depths of the eye, this blind spot is in the depths of life.

We must come to a full understanding of the state of being of the newborn child. Only then will the absolute necessity of rendering easy his initiation into life become evident. The newborn child must become the object of knowledgeable care. Even holding him requires the utmost gentleness, and he should not be moved except with great tenderness. We must understand that in the first moment, and even in the first month, the child should be kept very quiet. The infant ought to be left naked, warmed only by the air in the room itself, not clothed or wrapped in blankets, for he has little body heat with which to resist temperature change and clothing is of little help.

I do not want to insist on this argument here because I know every woman will tell me that I am ignoring the customary ways of caring for the child in different lands. To that charge I merely respond that I know all these various methods of child care because I have studied them in many different countries and have observed them with the deepest interest. And I have found these methods to be lacking in some respects. And, I must repeat, what is really lacking is the consciousness necessary to receive the newborn human in a worthwhile manner.

But if it is true that we do the best we can,

23

what is progress if not seeing that which we did not see before and doing that which we have never done, reaching for new things because they appear to be perfect and complete?

The fact is that the child is not understood very well anywhere. This ignorance is a consequence of the subconscious apprehension and annoyance we manifest toward him from the very first moments of his life, an instinctive defensiveness about our possessions, even if they are worth nothing. Our attitude develops logically from these beginnings, and we are obsessed with fears that the child will destroy the daily order of our lives or disfigure and dirty our homes. Yet when we have a child in the home, not only do we deal with him by rushing to save our things from destruction and even by fleeing the house to save our peace of mind, but we also suppress the child's so-called caprices so that he does not become a slave to them and develops finally into a well-bred child.

But in attempting to accomplish this, we commit serious error simply out of incomprehension and assess as capricious much of the child's behavior that is not capricious at all. For example, during the first year, and especially in the second, the child has a positive need to see objects always in their accustomed places and used for their customary purposes. If anyone disturbs this familiar order, the child is deeply offended;

he feels frustrated and defends himself by putting the objects back into their rightful places.

We have seen this in our schools, where even the smallest child demonstrates the need to put things where they belong. One child, for instance, stood looking at some sand that was scattered on the floor. His mother saw the sand and brushed it away, whereupon to her amazement he burst into tears, gathered the sand up and returned it to its original position. His mother then understood the reason for his tears but assumed them to be a kind of naughtiness.

The mother of another child felt warm one day, took off her coat and threw it over her arm. The child began to weep, and no one could understand why he would not calm down until she put her coat back on. Once again, what had disturbed the child was seeing an object in an unfamiliar position.

The adult assumes in such cases that by punishing a child he is correcting the child's defects. *But clearly it is useless to correct defects that the child will no longer have when he is an adult;* certainly adults do not weep when women remove their coats! We do not understand children's acts for themselves and instead continue to see them as forms of misbehavior. At least we ought to recognize that such "defects" will finally disappear and that they are not worth worrying about. When we begin to accept this approach to

25

the child, we begin to understand many things and to love the child with the little peccadilloes that he will one day lose as a complex, rational adult.

Just one more example: I knew of a two-year-old whose nurse always bathed him in the same tub and in the same way. When she had to be away for a period of time, another nurse substituted for her. The child cried every time the new nurse tried to bathe him, and she was at a loss to know why. When the old nurse returned, she asked the child, "Why did you always cry? Wasn't she a nice lady?" The child replied, "No, because she bathed me backward." Where one had started with the head, the other started with the feet. The child's drive for order was a part of his life, and he defended it as best he could. Yet it is this drive that we often call "misbehavior" in a child.

3
THE
SPIRITUAL
EMBRYO

The newborn child should be seen as a "spiritual embryo"—a spirit enclosed in flesh in order to come into the world. Science, on the other hand, assumes that the new being comes with nothing. He is flesh but not spirit, for all that can be verified is the growth of tissues and organs that ultimately form a living whole. But this too is a mystery: is it possible that a complex, living body comes out of nothing?

The newborn child is at an impressionable point of departure. The child is born inert and stays inert for a long time, incapable of doing anything and requiring the same care as an invalid or a paralytic. Silent, he cannot make himself heard for quite a while except in sobs or screams of pain; then he can make us come running as we would to one who needs help. Only after a long period of time, months and even a year or more, does he cease to be an infirm creature and become a recognizable young human being. And again, only after months and years does his voice become that of a young human being.

The physical and psychological phenomenon of growth can be viewed as a process of incarnation. That is, growth is esentially a mysterious process in which a form of energy animates the inert body of the newborn child and gives to it the use of its limbs, the faculty of speech, the power to act and to express its own will: thus is man incarnate.

It is, in fact, important that the human child is born and remains helpless for so long a period of time, while the young of other animals, almost immediately after birth, or at least after a very short time, can sustain themselves, walk and even run behind the mother, can communicate in the manner of their species, no matter how weakly or imperfectly. Kittens can actually meow, lambs can in their small way bleat, foals neigh—weak voices, but the world resounds incessantly with the voices of newborn animals. The period of preparation is quick and easy. These creatures

are born, one might say, already animated with
the instincts which will determine their behavior.
Very shortly after birth, for example, the agile cat
is apparent in the tiger cub. The frolicsome kid
is on his feet from the moment of his birth.

Every creature that comes into the world is
not only a physical being, but has latent in it
functions which depend upon instinct. All instinct is manifest in movement and represents the
distinctive characteristics of the species. Animals,
it is said, are characterized by behavioral attributes rather than physical characteristics. It is
possible, then, to combine all those characteristics that could not be used to describe plant life,
and call them psychological characteristics. Psychological traits are apparent in animals from the
moment of birth; how, then, is it possible to
argue that the human infant is not similarly endowed? There is one scientific theory that ex-
plains animal movement as the accumulated past
experience of the species; why cannot human
characteristics be argued upon the same grounds?
For human beings have always walked erect, developed language and transmitted their experience to their posterity.

Somewhere among all these apparent contradictions there must be a hidden truth. Let me
pose an analogy based on the idea of human
goods and production. Some objects are rapidly
mass-produced by press or machine and are ex-

31

actly alike. Others are made slowly by hand, and
each is different from the other. The value of
handmade objects is that each carries the individual imprint of the artist who created it. This
analogy expresses to a degree the psychic distinction between man and animal, the latter being
like the mass-produced objects in which each
individual reproduces in itself the fixed and uni-
form characteristics of the species. Man, however, is "worked by hand," and each individual is
different from the other, having his own distinctive created spirit, as if he were a natural work of
art. Moreover, the work is slow and lengthy.
Before any external signs are manifested, there
must be an inner development that is not a
reproduction of a fixed type, but the dynamic
creation of a new type; the inner life is an enigma which produces an unpredictable result. Human development is always a lengthy and interi-
or process, exactly like that necessary to produce
the work of art that the artist, sequestered in the
intimacy of his studio, modifies and transforms
before he brings it before the public.

The process by which the human personality is formed is the hidden work of incarnation.
The helpless infant is an enigma. The only thing
we know about him is that he could be anything,
but nobody knows what he will be or what he
will do. His helpless body contains the most
complex mechanism of any living creature, but it

is distinctly his own. Man belongs to himself, and his special will furthers the work of incarnation. Musicians, singers, artists, athletes, tyrants, heroes, criminals, saints—all are born in the same way, but each carries within him the enigma of his own special development that motivates his unique activity in the world.

The phenomenon of the child's helplessness at birth has been the subject of philosophical speculation, but it has never attracted the attention of medical practitioners, psychologists or educators. It has remained one of those self-evident facts one simply takes for granted. Yet much survives from this period of helplessness, locked and buried within the subconscious, and the effects of infancy can generate grave psychological consequences in the daily life of the child. Those who have assumed that not only the body of the infant is passive, but the self is inert and empty of life, have thought erroneously. In the face of the magnificent but late development of the child, the adult is equally in error who assumes that such development has come about solely through his care and upbringing. Such an assumption generates a sense of duty and responsibility; the parent sees himself literally as the force which animates the child and his inner life, therefore he acts externally upon the child as one would upon a creative piece of work, giving suggestions and directives in order to develop

33

intelligence, sensitivity and will. The adult ultimately attributes to himself powers nearly divine
and ends up believing that he occupies a place
in the child's life quite like that of God in
Genesis: "And God created man in his own
image and likeness."

Pride is the worst sin of man, and his eleva-
tion of himself to divine status has been the
cause of great suffering to his descendants. Indeed, if the child does carry within himself the
key to his locked selfhood, if he does display
developmental directions and certain psychic
gifts, then his attempts to express them openly
are potential and tentative. At this point, the
untimely intervention of the adult, exalted by his
illusions of power, could cancel out these striv-
ings and frustrate their inner realization. Truly,
it is possible for the adult to negate a human
design ordained at birth; perhaps this was the
course of things as, generation to generation, the
incarnate spirit of man became deformed. The
real problem lies in the fact that the child possesses a psychic life, even when he cannot
manifest it because the immense difficulty of re-
alizing it must be struggled with internally over
such a long period of time.

This idea reveals a striking truth—a hidden
imprisoned spirit is born and grows, animating
little by little the passive flesh, calling forth the
voice of the will, coming into the light of con-

sciousness with the force of a living creature being born into the world. But in the new environment another being of enormous power awaits it and ultimately dominates it. In the new environment there is no awareness or acceptance of the fact of the human incarnation. No protection is provided for the fragile newcomer, nor is any aid offered him in his difficult undertaking. Everything becomes an obstacle.

The child thus incarnate is a spiritual embryo which must come to live for itself in the environment. But like the physical embryo, the spiritual embryo must be protected by an external environment animated by the warmth of love and the richness of value, where it is wholly accepted and never inhibited.

Having once understood this, the adult must change his attitude toward the child. The figure of the child as spiritual embryo confronts us and imposes new responsibilities. That tender, graceful little being, whom we adore and whom we overwhelm with material things and who is almost like a toy to us, must inspire reverence in us. *Multa debetur puero reverentia.* (We must revere the young.)

The incarnation comes at the cost of great inner difficulty, and around this creative work unfolds a drama that has yet to be written. It is almost impossible to conceive of a will that does not yet exist, but that must ultimately control the passive body in order to animate and discipline it. At the moment that tentative, delicate life flowers into consciousness, putting the senses in contact with the environment, the muscles are activated in the perpetual effort of realization. This inner effort of the child must remain sacred. This labored manifestation must find us sympathetic, because in this creative period the future personality of the man is determined. Given such a responsibility, it is our duty to attempt to understand, also with the aid of scientific means, the psychic needs of the child and to prepare a vital environment for him. This is the first principle of a science a long time in the development, and it is a science with which the intelligent adult must collaborate, for there will be a vast amount of work before the last word can be said about human development.

4
THE
LOVE
TEACHERS

The child is extremely sensitive to everything he feels from the adult and wants to obey in every respect. Indeed, we have no idea to what degree or how perfectly he is ready to obey us always, yet it is this which characterizes him. One child, for example, put his slipper on the bed, and his mother said to him: "Don't do that; slippers are dirty," and brushed off the bedspread with her hand. After that, whenever the child saw a slipper, he exclaimed, "It's dirty!" and went to the bed to brush it off.

What more could we want? The child is sensitive and impressionable to such a degree that the adult ought to monitor everything he says and does, for everything is literally engraved in the child's mind. He is all obedience, because obedience is his life, and he loves and venerates the adult from whose mouth comes all the wisdom necessary to guide him in life. We ought, therefore, to think how an apparent bit of misbehavior might be a vital act or a profound defense, and to keep in mind that the child is always ready to love and obey us.

Children love adults; this is how we must know them. Yet we always speak of how much parents and teachers love children. People even speak of how children must be taught to love their mothers, fathers, teachers—indeed, everything and everyone. And who are these instructors who would teach the child to love? Those who judge as misbehavior all the child's activities and who deal with them punitively? No adult can become a teacher of love without a special effort, without opening the eyes of his consciousness in order to see a world more vast than his own.

Yes, children love adults deeply. When the child goes to bed he must do so in the company of someone he loves. But the person he loves thinks: "This nonsense must stop. We'll spoil him if we stay close to him before he goes to sleep." Or: "If the baby wants to come to the table with us, and cries if we do not let him, then we must pretend we're not going to eat!" But the child only wants to be present when his loved ones eat, even though he may only be a toddler whose diet is still fairly restricted. He will stop crying if he is brought to the table. If he does cry at table, it is because nobody pays any attention to him. *He wants to be part of the group.*

Who else weeps out of the intense desire to be with us while we eat? And how sadly we will say someday, "Nobody cries now to have me near him while he falls asleep. Everybody thinks of himself and falls asleep remembering what happened during the day, but nobody thinks of me." Only a child remembers and says every night, "Don't leave me; stay with me!" and the adult answers, "I can't; I have so much to do, and anyway, what kind of nonsense is this?" and thinks that the child must be corrected or he will make everyone a slave of his love!

Sometimes a child awakens in the morning and goes to wake his parents, who would rather sleep; everyone complains about this kind of thing. But the child who slips from his bed is a pure being who does that which everyone ought to do. When the sun rises everyone should get up, but the parents are still sleeping. The child goes to them almost as if to say, "You must learn to live well; come, the morning wakes us." But

the child is no teacher; he looks at his parents
only because he loves them. Once awake, he is
impelled toward those he loves, through rooms
that are still dark, closed to the light. He goes,
stumbling perhaps, but unafraid of the shadows
and the half-closed doors, approaches his parents
and touches them lightly. Most often they say,
"Don't wake me up in the morning," and the
child responds, "I didn't wake you up; I only
kissed you!" And the parents think of ways to
remonstrate with him. But how often does it
happen in life that someone, just awakened,
wants to come to us, despite every difficulty, not
to wake us up but simply to see and kiss us?

We say that this kind of misbehavior must
be corrected; these facts of love count for nothing with us.

The child who loves wakes not only to the
morning but also to his father and mother who
sleep too much and often are asleep throughout
their lives. We all have the tendency to sleep
through things, yet, with the coming of a child,
there is a new being who awakens us and keeps
us awake with means that are not ours, a being
who operates in a way different from our way
and who appears every morning as if to say,
"Look, there is another life; you can live better
than you do."

We can always live better, because man has

a tendency to laziness. It is the child who can help him to rise. If the adult does not make the attempt, he is lost; little by little, he hardens and finally becomes insensitive.

5
THE
NEW
EDUCATION

The idea that education must begin at birth has been a consistent theme in the preceding discussion, although the question of how has not yet been dealt with. The question would apppear to be absolutely theoretical and impracticable, or at least not as concrete as a discussion of the health needs of the child. There are, for instance, certain doctors who have worked out plans for a special school for children in the first year of life. They would undergo exercises for their arms and legs that would prepare them for the ordinary movements they would utilize later on. Certainly they are mistaken and do not take into account

the fact that the poor newborn child has enough
to do and is injured by such attempts at education. We need not, however, be limited by our
sensitivity to this fact, and can counter such
attempts with a clear statement of principle: To
conceive of the education of the newborn child
in that fashion is erroneous. It is clear that the
adult who exercises the limbs of the child substi-
tutes his own mode of action for that of the
child, thereby perpetuating a universal error. *The
adult ought never to mold the child after himself, but should leave him alone and work always
from the deepest comprehension of the child
himself.*

Physical movement ought to come from
within and be organized by the inner life of the
child. It is this organization that was described
earlier as incarnation. Muscles do not develop
correctly unless they do so at the service of the
will, for physical movement is the expression of
an operative will. We can do nothing but wait for
this inner life to organize itself. We must, however, encourage in ourselves every means of com-
prehending the process of development, for we
lack direct communication with the child, most
particularly language, and therefore we cannot in
any precise way understand him as an individual.
This crucial comprehension is acquired little by
little, but it must be founded in the certainty that
there is, indeed, something to observe.

Generally, we tend to consider the child as a physical vegetable or as a troublesome individual who requires a great deal of care and disturbs everybody else with his crying. We consign him to this kind of treatment for up to a year, ignoring his psychic development. Those religions that maintain that a human personality is already present in the infant are correct; Christians baptize the child in the belief that he already possesses a soul, thereby acknowledging his psychic life. Despite this, however, they do not take into consideration the latent individuality in a period of fundamental importance for the total development of the personality. An error is much more deleterious when it affects an individual in the process of his development than when it is committed upon someone who has already completed his inner development. In this sense, anything that inhibits the growth of the child is particularly grave because it can influence the entire construct of the personality that must ultimately emerge. We must understand, therefore, that this problem is of fundamental importance not only in education but in the history of mankind.

We must try to observe the elusive manifestations that demonstrate how the psychic life of the child develops from the moment of birth and acquires a recognizable pattern in the first months of life.

The small child, and also one who is a few

49

years old, is defined by educators as a *cera molle*
("soft wax"), which can be shaped in the appropriate way. Now the concept inherent in the
definition of *cera molle* is correct; the error lies
in the fact that the educator believes that he
must shape the child. On the contrary, the child
must shape *himself*; this is a basic principle, for
the child is truly self-animated even in the means
by which he expresses himself. The individual
adult, omnipotent master of these little beings,
can with a blind, barbaric and inopportune intervention erase the rough outlines of form that the
child begins to put upon his own "soft wax."
Indeed, to call such intervention evil would not
be too extreme.

There is a Japanese tale about the spirits of
dead children, which, having ascended into eternal life, worked very hard to build little towers
with a great many tiny pebbles. But evil demons
destroyed the little towers faster than the children could build them. This symbolically represents the damnation of the child.

At any rate, the actions of adults are exactly
the kind that, even if they are not consciously so,
are evil in their destructive effects upon all that
the child has so delicately and laboriously built
within himself. When the adult is not looking,
the child begins again, and the adult destroys
again. The struggle goes on until the child is

completely defenseless and can no longer speak or act for himself.

It is easy to understand then how important education is in such a delicate period—in fact, more important than in any period that follows. The adult must remain quite passive and never intervene in any blind or inopportune way so that he avoids becoming a destructive force. We can understand this in light of hell and the devil and their contrasting ideas: the divine power to create and the evil to destroy. As educators, we can choose the proper path, using our sensitivity to understand what action is necessary to help in the construction of the child. We must inhibit ourselves in order not to become destructive. The one who creates is the child; we do not. It is no easy matter to make this clear, for in the popular mind it is the adult who creates the new life. What must happen, therefore, is a kind of purification, whereby we liberate ourselves of the unseemly illusion of our omnipotence.

Having done this, we must try to understand the child's personality better. The first duty of the educator, whether he is involved with the newborn infant or an older child, is to recognize the human personality of the young being and respect it. We demonstrate a lack of respect toward the child when we do not allow him to be with us because he might annoy us. Just as we observe amenities in the adult world, so would it be no mistake to do so with the small child. If we are at dinner and the child is in another room and he weeps because he is left out, we have withheld the respect we would have given an adult. We must consider, as we would with any person for whom we have regard, that the child would "do us an honor" by being at table with us; we ought to be pleased by his presence and keep him near us. Some people believe that it is unhealthy for the child to eat adult food at adult hours, but we need not be too worried about this. All sorts of things can do him harm, and we let those go. Most of all, if we ignore him, we offend the child, and this we do without even begging his pardon.

The most marvelous aspect of the child is that he is quite an acute observer who sees things that we cannot imagine he can have seen. How peculiar, then, that we believe we must use bright colors, exaggerated gestures and loud voices to attract his attention. What we do not know is that the child has a great capacity for observation and absorbs many images, not only of things, but of actions. The child absorbs not only images of things but relationships among things, and is already greatly advanced when we are least aware of it. For example, one four-week-old infant, who had never been outside of the house in which he was born, had seen only two men, his father and his uncle, but always separately; then one day he saw them together. The child looked amazed and gazed at one and then the other for a long time; the two men stood quietly in front of the child in order to give him time to observe. Had the two men left the room or said something to distract him, the child would never have made any sense out of an experience that profoundly impressed him. The two men finally left, but slowly, so that he would have time to see each of them and persuade himself that they were two distinct persons. Here is an exercise in the adult's educating the child by helping him with his inner construction.

There are other telling examples of children who could not yet walk or talk. An adult was carrying a child of a few months in his arms. The child saw a painting of some fruit in the dining room; he looked at it and then imitated the gestures of eating. The child at this point drank only milk, but he had seen adults eating fruit. The adult who carried him, caught by his interest and enjoyment, stood with him before the painting until his interest waned. This adult was certainly what we can call an educator, allowing the child to complete his interior exercise, manifested by his imitation of adult actions.

Another example concerns a small child who saw some statues of ballet dancers in a hall and immediately began to dance. He had already seen people dance and had recognized the positions depicted in the statues.

Children are always attracted to the same objects in a room. If someone sets down something that was not there before, the child will immediately see the new object and ask what it is. One girl, being taken out to play one day, noticed a stone lying near a wall. The stone impressed her, and every time she went out, she was not satisfied unless she stopped to look at it.

There is no doubt that children love light and flowers and watching animals, which is understandable because we know that they are acute observers who can order the images of what they perceive. The child always acts to satisfy his passion for observation. He will, for example, watch closely the mouth of an individual adult who speaks to him, yet we often think that to claim the attention of a child it is necessary to shout or call him by name. This is not so, for instead of speaking, if we make small but distinct movements with our lips, the child will become very attentive. This is something which fascinates him, for what is developing in him is his awareness of a task he must accomplish—he is becoming sensitive to language. If one holds a child of four months near a person who makes only lip movements, the child will watch with great interest. Evidently these movements please him more than most things because they stimulate the imitative capacity that coincides with his necessary inner development.

Let us look at older children. I had the occasion to watch some Japanese fathers who demonstrated a deeper comprehension of children than we do. One was taking a walk with his two-year-old son, who suddenly sat down on the sidewalk. His father did not shout at him, "The sidewalk is dirty—get up!" but waited patiently until the little boy got up by himself to continue the walk. *Even this is the exercise of an educator, for the father submerged his dominant personality to that of the child by respecting his activity.* I saw another of these fathers standing with his legs spread apart so that his child could run in and out between them. The poor man even managed to look dignified in that position. I greatly admired the wisdom which many peoples have acquired, or perhaps already knew, from their traditions; we, on the other hand, seem anxious only that the child become an adult in society.

I watched one mother, who, as a matter of fact, had taken one of our courses, while she led her child through a street in Milan. The air was filled with the sound of bells and the child wanted to stop to listen, but his mother denied him that joy and forced him, reprovingly, to continue walking. It is not easy to persuade the adult to adopt an attitude of consistent passivity

with regard to his child, yet it is absolutely
necessary that the individual adult seek to acquire an understanding of infantile necessity and
curb his particular vanity as a molder of the
child's life. Equally necessary is the self-
education of each particular inner being.

These days we seem preoccupied solely with
the need of the child for fresh air and sunshine,
two very excellent things, but only for the body.
But if the sun's rays suffice the body, in the
psychic world, so to speak, there is not a single
ray of sun. It is the inner construction peculiar to
each child—slow, fragile and crucial—that the
adult destroys with his power and his blindness.

The adult must acquire the sensitivity to
recognize all the child's needs; only thus can he
give the child all the help that is necessary. If we
were to establish a principle, it would be that
what is necessary is the child's participation in
our lives, for in that period in which he must
learn to act, he cannot learn well if he does not
see how, just as he could not learn language if he
were deaf. To extend to the child this hospitality,
that is, to allow him to participate in our lives, is
difficult, but costs nothing; it depends solely on
the emotional preparation of the adult. The child
who does not act, asks nothing; his presence is
practically a spiritual one. But the extension of
adult hospitality is opposed by the prejudice,
supported tyrannically and cruelly by health

science, that a child must get a great deal of sleep, like a vegetable. Why force him to sleep? If we allow him to stay awake as much as he likes and we keep him near us, we will see that he needs to sleep a great deal less.

The prejudice that condemns children to sleep is very popular among northern peoples and is without any foundation, but we accept it without argument. One time a child came to me saying that he wanted to see something very beautiful, of which he had heard much talk—the stars. He had never seen them because he had to go to bed very early. It is easy to understand that the child condemned to sleep must find the inner work of construction extremely fatiguing because he is forced to struggle with the adult, who destroys the building process and for the most part condemns him to sleep.

Teaching charity, Christ said, "Do not put out a smoking candle"—that is, "Do not bother putting out a candle that is already extinguishing itself." We can borrow this principle of charity and apply it to education: "Do not erase the designs the child makes in the soft wax of his inner life." This is the greatest responsibility for the adult who educates the child who is in the process of constructing himself.

The fundamental educational concept is that we must not become obstacles to the development of the child. Knowing what we must do is neither fundamental nor difficult, but to comprehend which presumptions and which vain prejudices we must rid ourselves of in order to be able to educate our children is most difficult.

6
MY
METHOD
IN GENERAL

It is clear that in the older and more familiar forms of education the child was not dealt with in terms of his true being but rather was forced to adapt himself to a form of society peculiar to the adult and therefore contrary to his own nature in the first years of life. The child was only a "future" and did not represent a "becoming"; he was not, therefore, really taken into account until the day he became a man.

Yet the child, like all human beings, has a personality of his own. He carries within himself the beauty and dignity of a creativity that can never be erased and for which his spirit, pure and sensitive, exacts from us a most delicate kind of care. We must not only be occupied with his body, so tiny and fragile, and we must not only think of feeding him, washing him and dressing him with the greatest of care. That no man lives on bread alone is never so apparent as in childhood; material things are the least important in that period and can be used for degrading purposes at any age. Slavery in children, as well as in adults, elicits feelings of inferiority and total lack of dignity.

The social ambience that we have created does not suit the child; he does not understand it because he is kept apart from it, and, not knowing how to adapt to that from which he is excluded, he is entrusted to a school that very often becomes for him a prison. Now we see clearly the fatal consequences of schools where outmoded teaching methods are practiced: children suffer not only physically but morally. Here, then, is the fundamental problem of education: until now the education of character has been neglected.

Elsewhere, even in the family, we find the same error in principle: everyone thinks only of the child's tomorrow, of his future existence; no one ever concerns himself with the present, where so much is required of the child to live. More often than not, the modern family is completely involved in the child's physical life; reasonable diet, bathing, proper dress, play in the fresh air are the only criteria for assessing his progress.

But of all the necessities the child requires, the one most often neglected is that which defines his humanity: his spiritual needs. The human being who lives in the child remains hidden. Only the forces and energy necessary for the child to defend himself from us are revealed: sobs, screams, misbehavior, shyness, disobedience, lying, egoism and destructiveness. We commit the gravest of errors if we consider these means of defense the essential elements of the child's character. And when we make this mistake, we then believe it our duty to eliminate these characteristics with the greatest stringency, sometimes by means of physical punishment. Yet, these reactions on the part of the child are often indications of moral illness, or sometimes of nervous disorders, the consequences of which can be felt for the rest of the child's life.

We all know that this period of development is the most important in one's life, that moral starvation or spiritual disease can be as fatal for man as starvation of the body. Consequently, childhood education is mankind's most crucial problem.

We are bound, therefore, to make the most conscientious attempts to understand even the smallest effacement of the child's spirit and to establish close rapport with the world of chil-

63

dren. Until now, we have almost enjoyed making pitiless judgments upon children who always appeared full of defects in the face of our abundant virtue, but now we must adopt a role that is a good deal more modest. This corresponds to Emerson's interpretation of the message of Jesus: "Childhood is an eternal Messiah, continually coming back to the arms of fallen man to pray for his return to Heaven." If we would only consider how absolute and urgent are the requirements of child care, we would perform a great service for the good of humanity.

No child can lead a regular life in the complex world of the adult. Indeed, it is well known that the adult, with his continual surveillance, his uninterrupted admonishment and his arbitrary commands, disturbs and impedes the child's development. In this fashion, all the vital energy in the process of germination is suffocated, and for the child but one thing remains: the intense desire to free himself as soon as possible from everything and everyone.

We must, therefore, quit our roles as jailers and instead take care to prepare an environment in which we do as *little as possible* to exhaust the child with our surveillance and instruction. However much the environment corresponds to the needs of the child, by so much will our roles as teachers be limited. We must, however, keep one idea clearly in mind—to give a child liberty is not to abandon him to himself or to neglect him. The help we give must not amount to a passive indifference to all the difficulties he will encounter; rather, we must support his development with prudent and affectionate care. Furthermore, even in the preparation of the child's environment we are faced with a serious task, for in a sense we must create a new world—the world of childhood.

If we just put out the tiny furniture children require, we see immediately that they order their activity in an extraordinary fashion. Everything they do is willed; they get along perfectly well by themselves, without any danger, because they know what they want. In children, the drive for activity is almost stronger than that for food, although we rarely see it because they lack it in their present forced environment. If we give them the right environment, we see little unhappy nuisances transformed into happy, active children. The proverbial housewrecker becomes the most attentive custodian of the objects which surround him; the noisy and disorganized child is transformed into a tranquil and orderly being. For if the child lacks the external means to adapt, he has no way to utilize the great energy that is his. Moreover, he is impelled instinctively toward activity that utilizes all his energies because in this way he can perfect his faculties. Everything depends on this.

Today, of course, we are all familiar with
those things that are designed with the purpose
of serving the child's intellectual development. It
is possible to find graceful, tiny furniture, brightly colored and so light that the pieces turn over if
the child bumps into them—a quality that also
makes it possible for him to move them about
with ease. Spots show up clearly because of the
light colors, and this makes it possible for the tot
to see his responsibility immediately and to learn
the simple remedy of soap and water. Children
always find favorite places for themselves and
make themselves comfortable in some fashion
that pleases them, but light furniture tends to
exaggerate any abrupt movement by the noise it
makes. As a result of this, the child develops an
awareness of his bodily movement. One can also
get tiny objects made of glass or porcelain; the
child learns that if he lets them drop, they will
break and will be lost forever. The unhappiness
this causes him is his worst punishment.

The loss of a prized possession causes terrible pain for a child. Who has not felt impelled to
console a red-faced, weeping child in front of a
broken vase? But from that point on, the child
will exert every effort of will to walk steadily
when he carries a fragile object.

The environment itself will teach the child,
if every little error he makes is manifest to him,
without the intervention of a parent or teacher,

who should remain a quiet observer of all that happens. Little by little, it will seem to the child that he hears the silent language of objects advising his actions: "Pay attention, look! I am a newly varnished end table; don't scratch me or make me dirty!" The aesthetics, too, both of things and of the environment itself, encourage attentiveness in the active child; for this reason, everything ought to be attractive. Dustcloths ought to be multi-colored, brushes brightly colored and soap interestingly shaped. Attractive objects invite the child to touch them and then to learn to use them; he will be attracted to a brightly colored cloth and learn that it is used to dust tables, or to the brush for his clothes, or to the soap with which he must wash his hands. In this fashion, beautiful things will attract him from every corner and instruct him practically by themselves. Now it is no longer the teacher who says to the child entrusted to her, "Carl, brush yourself off," or, "John, wash your hands." Any child who is self-sufficient, who can tie his shoes, dress or undress himself, reflects in his joy and sense of achievement the image of human dignity, which is derived from a sense of independence.

The delight that children find in working impells them to attack everything with an enthusiasm that is almost excessive. If they shine a doorknob, they work at it so long that it gleams

67

like a mirror; even the simplest tasks such as
dusting or sweeping will be undertaken with extreme care and attention. Apparently, it is not
the completion of a given task that inspires them
but the fact that it utilizes their latent energies; it
is this utilization that determines the duration of
the activity.

The child is not made happy by the repetition of these activities, but he learns to do them
with great competence. We have seen very young
children dress and undress themselves, do up
their own buttons, tie knots and bows, set the
table perfectly and wash the dishes and glasses.
Their superabundance of energy also manifests
itself in the fact that the child uses what he has
learned for the benefit of other children who
have not achieved as much. I have seen a child
put on a smock for a smaller friend and tie his
shoelaces. Another child wiped up the floor when
a younger child spilled his soup.

If a child washes the dishes, he does so for
himself and for others who have dirtied them; if
he sets the table, he works for the good of many
others who have not shared the work with him.
Yet the child does not consider work done for
others as deserving a reward; it is the work itself
that rewards the most ambitious child. One day,
I saw a little girl sitting sadly in front of a plate
of hot soup without saying a word to anyone.
Someone had promised her that she could set the

table and then forgotten. The disappointment had silenced her hunger; her hurt feelings were stronger than her empty stomach.

In this fashion, then, does the child's external social behavior develop; he has an end that he understands perfectly well and that can be easily attained. By putting him within the framework of this environment, we give him the freedom to reach his end. Certainly true interest has very deep roots; the child operates in his fashion only to assuage his drive for activity and to satisfy the demands of his development. There must, however, be a simple, clear aim in order that his drives can be satisfied. A child will wash his hands countless times, not because they are dirty, but because he has at hand the physical objects that recall a progressive series of necessary secondary actions—carrying and pouring water, handling the soap and the towel. Sweeping the floors, changing the water in the flower vases, putting the little tables back in order, making the beds, setting the table for dinner—all these are rational activities that organize his physical exercise. Anyone who has had to do housework and has experienced the subsequent fatigue knows how much sheer movement is necessary to complete it. Especially today people talk a great deal about the necessity for gymnastics and physical exercise; here, then, are some exercises—not the

69

usual mechanical ones, but those that can be
done for a clear and apparent reason.

Yet even these activities, which the children
carried through with much gaiety and care and
which agreeably surprised all our visitors to the
Children's House, do not represent the essential
things. They are just a beginning and constitute
the least important level of childhood activities.

Thinkers and scientists are well known for
giving the impression of being so deeply involved
in thought that they are removed from the world
itself. Everyone knows those anecdotes about
how Newton forgot to eat and how Archimedes,
undisturbed by the din of battle in the conquest
of Syracuse, was surprised in the midst of his
mathematical calculations by the enemy. Yet, it
is precisely these anecdotes that indicate a human characteristic that overshadows the capacity
for deep thought. The great discoveries that have
fostered the progress of humanity have arisen
not so much from the culture or knowledge of
scientists as from their total power of concentration, their near-isolation from the world.

If the child found his area of activity corre-
spondent to his inner needs, he would reveal to
us even more that is necessary for his development. He seeks rapport with the type of human
beings who surround him, and he finds it.

But there are individual inner needs, for
which, while the child has buried himself in his

own special work, there must be complete solitude and a separation from everything and everyone. No one can help us to achieve the intimate isolation by which we find our secret worlds, so mysterious, rich and full. If others intervene, it is destroyed. This degree of thought, which we attain by freeing ourselves from the external world, must be fed by the inner spirit, and our surroundings cannot influence us in any way other than to leave us in peace.

Great or exceptional men exhibit the ability to achieve this degree of profound thought, and it is their source of inner strength. There are great men who, from this power of thought, have derived the faculty of influencing masses of people with a quiet thoughtfulness and infinite benevolence. There are men who, after a prolonged absence from the world of affairs, feel obliged to resolve the great problems of mankind while with infinite patience they support the weaknesses and imperfections of their peers, who have themselves succumbed to hatred and aggression. Furthermore, we see that there exists a strict relationship between manual labor and deep concentration of the spirit. At first glance these might appear to be opposed, but they are profoundly compatible, for the one is the source of the other. The life of the spirit prepares the dynamic power for daily life, and, on its side, daily life encourages thought by means of ordi-

71

nary work. The physical energy expended is continually renewed through the spirit. The man
who understands himself clearly responds to the
necessities of his inner life exactly as the body
responds to physical necessities such as hunger
and sleep. The mind that does not respond to its
own spiritual necessities runs the same risks as
the body that no longer responds to hunger
pangs or the need to rest.

But because we find in children this power
of thought, this immersion of the spirit within
itself, it is clear that this quality is not peculiar to
exceptional or particularly gifted people, but is a
universal human trait preserved in only a few
people in their maturity.

If we consider these flickering powers of
concentration in children, we must move to a
different area than that considered in the discussion of useful work. An object that is not in the
least useful will attract the immediate attention
of a child. He will occupy himself with it and
manipulate it in every possible way. Often his
manipulations will not be very orderly; often he
will destroy what he began the moment before
and will have to begin at the beginning again.
These movements will be repeated so many times
that the task does not appear to be performed
with particular enthusiasm, but we are viewing a
special phenomenon. The first time I discovered
this aspect of the child's character, I was stu-

pefied, and asked myself if I had not found
myself in the presence of an extraordinary fact, a
new and marvelous mystery, for many psychological theories crumbled before my eyes. It was
believed—and I believed it too—that children
were incapable of fixing their attention on any
object for very long. Yet before me, a four-year-
old girl, with every indication of the deepest
attention, was putting cylinders of various di-
mensions into a wooden frame. She put them in
with the greatest care, and when there were none
left, she took them out in order to put them right
back in and continued in this fashion seemingly
without end. I began to read a story. When she
had repeated her little task more than fourteen
times, I sat down at the piano and invited the
other children to sing. The little girl continued
her useless labor without moving, without raising
her eyes, completely oblivious to everything that
went on around her. All at once, she stopped,
got up, smiling and content, her eyes shining.
She seemed happy, rested and smiling, as children do when they awake to the beneficent sun.

From that time on, I observed these same
manifestations many more times. When the children had completed an absorbing bit of work,
they appeared rested and deeply pleased. It almost seemed as if a road had opened up within
their souls that led to all their latent powers,
revealing the better part of themselves. They ex-

73

hibited a great affability to everyone, put themselves out to help others and seemed full of good will. Then it would happen that one of them would quietly approach the teacher and whisper to her, as if confiding a great secret, "I'm a good boy!"

This observation has already been found valuable by others, but it is particularly useful to me. I took what happened within the children to be a law, and this made it possible for me to resolve completely the problem of education. It was clear to me that the concept of order and the development of character, of the intellectual and emotional life, must derive from this veiled source. Thereafter, I set out to find experimental objects that would make this concentration possible, and carefully worked out an environment that would present the most favorable external conditions for this concentration. And that is how my method began.

Certainly here lies the key to all pedagogy: to learn to recognize precious moments of concentration in order to utilize them for the teaching of reading, writing, storytelling and, later, grammar, arithmetic, foreign language and so on. Moreover, psychologists agree that there is a single method of teaching; one must sustain in the student the deepest interest and a lively and consistent attention. Education demands, then, only this: the utilization of the inner powers of the child for his own instruction. Is it possible? It is not only possible, it is necessary. Attention must be stimulated gradually in order to develop the powers of concentration. One must begin with objects that appeal to the senses, that are easily recognizable and that will interest the children: cylinders of various sizes and of colors arranged according to the spectrum, various distinct sounds, rough surfaces that are recognizable tactily. Later we introduce the alphabet, writing, reading, grammar, design, more complex operations in mathematics, history and science. This is how the child's knowledge is built.

As a result, the work of the new teacher is made somewhat delicate and difficult. Whether the child will find his own way to learning and perfection or whether he will be impeded depends on her. The most difficult thing to make clear to the new teacher is that because the child progresses, she must restrain herself and avoid giving directions, even if at first they are expected; she must understand well that she must exert no influence on either the formation or the discipline of her pupil, but that all her faith must repose in his latent powers. Certainly there is something that impels a teacher to advise very young students continually, to correct them or encourage them, to show them that she is superior in experience and culture; ultimately she must

75

be resigned to quelling every bit of vanity, or she will obtain no results.

A teacher must be assiduous, though, in compensating for her indirectness. She must conscientiously prepare an environment, placing educational materials about for some clear purpose and introducing the child with great care to the practical work of life. What is expected of her is the ability to distinguish the child who has chosen the right path from the one who has erred, and she must be imperturbable, ready to be there whenever she is called in order to attest to her love and confidence. To be always there—that is the point.

A teacher must be consecrated to bettering humanity. She must be like the Vestal who kept the sacred fire that others had lighted pure and free from contamination; the teacher must be dedicated to the fire of the inner life in all its purity. If this flame is neglected, it will be extinguished, never to be lighted again.

7
THE CHARACTER
OF
THE CHILD

It was no accident that I selected the title, "The Character of the Child." I do not intend the word *character* to mean solely the moral traits, but rather to denote that complex personality of the child, comprised not only of intellectual and physical manifestations, but a unity of these, one which cannot be analyzed from the psychological point of view. Above all, I want to take a look here at those forms of children's activities that so often are not examined carefully or, even more often, are not recognized as important.

It is possible to represent the execution of a given task through the functions of a curve. A horizontal line represents a state of rest; the space above the line, ordered activity; that below the line, disordered activity; the distance between the lines, the degree of the two activities; and the direction of the line, the course of time. In this fashion, we can represent any activity in regard to the duration of time and the degree of order as opposed to disorder. These data yield a curve representing the child's activity.[1]

In this fashion, we chart the activity of a child in the Children's House. He enters, is quiet for a moment, then goes to work. The curve is drawn upward into the space representing order. The child tires and, as a result, his activity is disorganized. The curve is then drawn through the line representing rest downward into the space representing disorder. After this, the child begins a new task. If, for example, he at first

[1] We know very well that it is impossible to measure the spiritual intensity, that is, the force of concentration. Further, it is absolutely impossible to pin down and measure succeeding states of concentration in a single person or those of a few persons involved in different occupations. It is not possible, in any absolute way, to reproduce with the curve any fixed values; rather it represents generally the fluctuation between order and disorder and the intensity of work. We need not even lose the view here that "intensity" can be measured only subjectively and by entirely external signs. These curves, therefore, are not really paradigms such as one might construct in an exact science or obtain as the result of a precise measurement. Our curves are merely schematic aids to facilitate the total view.

works with the cylinders, then takes up some crayons, works assiduously for some time, but then disturbs his neighbor, the curve must again be drawn downward. After this, he teases his companions, and the curve remains in the space designating disorder. Tiring of this, he takes up the bells, begins to work out the scale and becomes very absorbed; the curve again ascends into the space representing order. But as soon as he is finished, he is at a loss to occupy himself any further and goes to the teacher in a state of great irritation.

This curve cannot represent his approach to the work, a subject that I will take up shortly. The curve just described, however, is typical of those of a great many children who cannot seriously fix their attention on anything or occupy themselves at all, but who wander chaotically from one activity to the other and through whose hands passes in a few hours all the material that ought to serve for half the school year. This kind of disorganization is very common.

After a while—it can be days or weeks or months—we take a new activity curve for this same child and discover that he has gained the power of concentration.

There is also a curve that expresses fairly well the activity of the child who, although not seriously disorganized, is not yet completely orderly, and who maintains himself mid-way be-

81

tween the two. As soon as a child of this type
enters the school, he tends to take up some easy
task, perhaps domestic; later he drops it to find
some already familiar article among the educational materials in order to repeat some exercise
he already knows. But after a while, he looks
tired and unsure, and his line dips below the
plane representing rest. This pattern can be
verified not only for a single child but for an
entire class. In this case, what is the teacher
without practical experience to do? Is she to
conclude that the children, after having done so
much domestic or educational work, are tired
and that if a loss of concentration is indicated,
the fault is not hers?

If the teacher is rather soft-hearted and
knows the kind of psychological theory which is
so popular, she will certainly think that the children are absolutely exhausted from their labors
and will interrupt them. To divert them, she will
most certainly take them outside to play, where
they will run around madly in order to be taken
back into the class where they will be even more
restless than before. They will continue to
change occupations and a state of what is actually false tiredness will persist.

So many teachers draw the wrong conclusions from such situations. It is not true that a
child will be content with work just because he
has chosen it by himself! It is clear that children

select their work freely, but after a moment's attention, they get restless. The teachers claim that they try everything—rest, change of environment—but nothing succeeds and the children neither carry on their work nor are tranquil.

These teachers have studied the method to the letter, but they do not have the necessary faith and therefore have not respected the liberty of the child. Naturally, they could not have done less than heed every kind of advice and counsel put forward in the past. But they sought to interfere and to guide, and by doing so they have interrupted the natural development and destroyed where they would edify.

If, instead, a teacher respects the freedom of the child and has faith in him, if she has will enough to forget all she has learned, if she is modest enough not to consider her intervention essential, if she knows how to wait patiently, then she will see a complete change in the child. He is agitated until he seeks something within the depths of his mind that he has not yet found for himself.

But this is only possible if a child does not begin a new task even more difficult than the first. It must hold his entire attention; he must concentrate and consecrate his entire being, and at the same time, he must be free from everything that goes on around him. This is what we call the great work.

When the child is finished, certainly he will drop the object that was the instrument of his concentration. But the appearance of this child will be totally different from that of false tiredness. If he was tired earlier, now his eyes will shine and he will appear very rested; he seems moved by a new force and reanimated by a torrent of energy. This is the work cycle, which is composed of two parts: the first is the pure and simple preparation that introduces the child to the work and constructs the road to the second part, to the true great work.

The child is rested after the great work; indeed, one could say that only then is he truly rested. His beaming serenity and peace of mind tell us clearly that he is in possession of a new truth. Such a child shows no symptom of fatigue, but rather the physical signs of abundant vitality, not too different from the way we look after a particularly satisfying meal or a bath. These two are certainly forms of work, but far from diminishing our energies, they renew us; thus, there are psychic forms of work that give force to the spirit. Because the child can find repose in it, we must make the great work possible for him.

We ought to consider what it really means to rest. For us, rest does not mean utter sloth. Our muscles are not rested if we remain immobile, but rather when we work them easily. In this way, we find rest in intellectual labor that gives spiritual strength.

Life is mysterious. A teacher would never be respected for saying, "I will give this child this or that piece of work to give him energy." But this is the only way to reach him. Only the voice of life can choose the work that the child truly needs. Therefore, it is enough that the teacher respects this mysterious process and knows to wait with faith.

A child rested in this fashion is happy and friendly; he may even want to chat confidently with his teacher. It is as if his spirit is open and he seeks the teacher because only now does he recognize her superiority. Only now does he see in his surroundings things that before had completely escaped him. Without a doubt he has become richer, more receptive and motivated toward the group. In order to produce the energy to act on his new discoveries, he must collect himself. A teacher who would teach a child morally weak and starved finds no response, neither confidence nor obedience; even if, despite everything, such teaching were possible, it would be an imperfect, exhausting process.

All of this may seem odd, yet we must face the fact that we have dealt badly with the child. To have faith in someone or to obey him is not an external sign of inner necessity, and we have attempted to encourage these external manifestations in the child without giving him the chance to develop his inner forces and become master of himself. Instead of frustrating the child's development, our task is precisely to set him upon the road to his inner being.

The more the capacity to concentrate is developed, the more often the profound tranquility in work is achieved, then the clearer will be the manifestation of discipline within the child. Those teachers who arrive at this point in their educational methods have developed special expressions. For instance, one might ask the other, "How are your classes going? Are they organized yet?" And the other might respond, "Not yet." Or another might say, "Do you remember that boy who was so disorderly? Well, now he has pulled himself together." Teachers who agree with each other in this fashion already know what will happen; the rest comes by itself.

A single instance will form the discipline of a child, and self-disciplined children are on the way to a natural psychic development. Children who reach this stage become very work-oriented, so much so that they do not know how to be without something to do, and they will not even remain idle when they are waiting for someone; they are thoroughly disposed to activity.

The more that goes into this development, the briefer will be the period of false tiredness, while the period of tranquility that follows work will be lengthened, providing more time for the child to absorb what he has done. This is a tranquility of a thoroughly special nature—an active repose, so to speak—and, in the meanwhile, a work goes on within the child that no longer has any relationship with the outside world. The child is inwardly at peace, watches what is going on around him, arranges a few small details and makes a few discoveries.

Concentration consists of three distinct periods: preparation, the great work itself that involves some physical object, and a third period of inner activity in which the child achieves great contentment and clarity. A glimmer of this clarity is reflected externally, for the child sees things he has never seen before. There is an attendant phenomenon: the child becomes extraordinarily obedient and develops an almost inconceivable patience, which is rather surprising since he has received little formal instruction in obedience or patience.

A child who cannot keep his balance dares neither to walk nor to use his arms for fear of falling; he goes forward only uncertainly. But if he can learn to keep his balance, he will run, jump and turn right and left. The same is true for the psychic life. The child who has no spiritual balance and cannot collect his thoughts has no mastery over himself; can he yield to another's will without the danger of "falling"? How can he obey another's will if he cannot submit to his own will? Obedience is nothing more than a form of spiritual dexterity that presupposes internal equilibrium. This obedience arises from strength and is best expressed through the term *adaptation*. Biologists agree that it requires a great deal of strength to adapt to a given environment. Of what, then, consists this adaptation of which they speak? It is a kind of strength that permits the individual to conform in a manner corresponding to the determinative factors of the environment and to cultivate those mechanisms and functions that respond to whatever surrounds him. But before such forces can be put into action, before they can give rise to action, they must exist in themselves, for they cannot be called into being simply because necessity demands it. Horticulturists understand well that forced growth weakens the plant.

Because of this, children must be thoroughly strong beings and must possess spiritual equilibrium in order to be able to obey. In nature, a robust organism can adapt itself to circumstance; in similar fashion will the strong spirit obey and know to adapt itself to everything.

It is necessary, then, to give the child the possibility of developing according to the laws of his nature, so that he can become strong, and, having become strong, can do even more than we dared hope for him. How much has the child developed who has exercised to a degree the essential function of his spirit (concentration) in peace and freedom! All the rest comes as a consequence—he has acquired the mastery of his body, he can move as he wills and he knows how to watch himself. We can see he has arrived at this mastery by the fact that he is capable of being perfectly quiet. The mastery that a child can attain is often superior to that of an adult. But we must not forget how he has achieved this development and the role played by the environment.

I must repeat that it is not that I first posed these principles and then shaped my educational method around them. To the contrary, only the immediate observation of children whose freedom was respected revealed some of the laws of their inner being that I understand to be of universal value. These same children have sought the way to strength and have found it with the surest of instincts.

8
THE
CHILD'S
ENVIRONMENT

The tremendous influence that the environment has upon living creatures has already been well substantiated in the biological sciences; the materialist theories of evolution describe how dramatically the environment acts upon the lives and forms of creatures, changing or transforming them. Despite the fact that the materialist theory has already been abandoned, the importance of understanding the environment in which plant and animal life develops is attested to by the intensity of the study devoted to it. Although it is not possible to discuss all the various theoreticians, this conclusion is especially justifiable on

the basis of the work of Fabre, who imparted
new insights into the lives of insects precisely by
studying the environment in which they habitually live. On the basis of this work in biology, it is
certain that no living creature can be clearly
understood unless he is observed in his natural
environment.

When we turn to man, we see that rather
than adapting to the environment, he creates an
environment to suit himself. Man lives in a social environment, and within this environment,
certain determinative spiritual forces are at work—
the interrelationships among men that constitute
their social lives. The man who does not live in
an adaptive environment can neither develop his
faculties normally nor learn to know himself.
One of the central principles of modern educational theory deals precisely with the necessity of
developing the social instinct of the child and
encouraging his drive to live with his peers.

In the meantime, there is no environment
into which the child fits because he lives in a
world of adults. This inequity has certain characteristic consequences in the lives of modern children. For instance, because of the difference in
size between the child and the objects that surround him, he sees no relationship between himself and them and cannot achieve a natural development.

This environmental imbalance is crucial not

only because of the size difference but because of the effects of this on the agility of the child's movements. Imagine an amazingly dexterous juggler performing his tricks—if I were to try to imitate him, he might wonder what I thought I was doing because it would not be possible to copy him. If I tried to do so in slow motion, surely he would lose patience. Do we behave otherwise toward our children? I would give one simple piece of advice to every mother: let your three- and four-year-old children wash themselves, undress themselves, eat by themselves exactly as they want to!

If we had to live just one day in an environment such as the one we prepare for our children, I believe we also would find it painfully uncomfortable. We would have to waste all our energy in defending ourselves, battling always with the same words: "No, leave me alone, I don't want to!" We would end up by bursting into tears because there was no other means of defense. Yet mothers tell me: "That child is impossible! He doesn't want to get up, he won't nap even for a little while, and he's always saying, 'I won't, I won't!' No child should say that all the time!"

But if these mothers prepared an environment at home for the child that conformed to his size, to his energy and to his psychic faculties, the child would be at liberty and a great step

95

would have been taken toward the resolution of the educational problem—the child would have his own environment.

A school, a place built for children, must have furniture and equipment scaled to the proper size and adapted to their physical strength, so that they can move it with the same ease with which we move the furniture in our homes.

Here, then, are fundamental principles: the furniture must be light and arranged in such a fashion that the child can easily move it, and the pictures must be hung at a level that permits the child to look at them comfortably. We must apply these principles to all surrounding objects, starting with the rugs and ending with the vases, dishes and other such things. The child must be able to use everything he comes across in the house and he must be able to do the ordinary tasks of everyday life—sweep, vacuum the rugs, wash and dress himself. The objects surrounding the child should look solid and attractive to him, and the "house of the child" should be lovely and pleasant in all its particulars; for beauty in the school invites activity and work, as adults know that domestic beauty nourishes domestic unity. It is almost possible to say that there is a mathematical relationship between the beauty of his surroundings and the activity of the child; he will make discoveries rather more voluntarily in a gracious setting than in an ugly one.

Children intuit these things very well by
themselves. A little girl from one of our schools
in San Francisco went one day to visit a public
school and immediately noticed that the desks
were dusty. She said to the teacher, "Do you
know why your children don't dust and instead
leave everything in a mess? Because they don't
have pretty dustcloths. I wouldn't want to clean
without them."

The furnishings that the child will use must
be washable. The motive for this is not just a
hygienic one; the real reason is that washable
furniture supplies the occasion for the kind of
work children do very willingly. They learn to
pay attention, wash off the marks and in time
become habituated to being responsible for
cleaning everything around them.

People always tell me to put rubber stops
under the legs of the furniture to lessen the
noise; I prefer the noise because it signals any
abrupt motion. Children do not move in a very
orderly fashion and they do not know how to
control their movements very well; in contrast to
ours, their muscles produce disordered movement precisely because they have not yet learned
physical order and economy.

In the "house of the child" every abrupt
motion reveals itself by the noise of the chair and
the table, and finally the child becomes aware of
his body. There must also be a certain number of

97

fragile objects—glasses, plates, vases and so
forth. Now certainly adults will exclaim, "How
come? Put glasses in the hands of three- and
four-year-old children! They will surely break
them!" By this comment they place more importance on the glass than on the child; an object
worth a few cents seems more precious than the
physical training of their children.

In a house that is truly his, a child tends to
be as well behaved as possible and seeks to
control his movements; in this fashion, he starts
on the road to perfection without external prod-
ding. We can see a new joy and dignity in him,
and sometimes an ineffable decorum, showing
that the road is natural for him and that he loves
it. Because, really, what lies ahead for the three-
year-old child? Growth. He will become a man;
we must do everything to help him perfect himself. In other words, we must exercise him in the
things he must do, for exercise gives rise to development. The child is delighted by washing his
hands not so much for the pleasure of washing
itself as for the work that is necessary for com-
pleting an action; already action is life, and this
is the source of all of his powers.

What should we do in the face of this life
that is developing and that tries to perfect itself
through work and energy? Often we impede its
realization with all of our strength. In many

schools, for example, desks and chairs are fixed
to the floor. The children are lively and often
their movements are clumsy, but it does not
occur to them that this could ruin the furniture
were it not fixed. By fixing the furniture we do
achieve a certain order, but the children will
never acquire order in their physical activity. We
might give a child a metal cup or plate that he
can throw to the floor without breaking, but by
doing so, we have tempted him diabolically.
Thus, we seek to hide that which is bad simply
by not looking at it, while the only one truly
involved, the child, cannot be held accountable
for his inadequacies. And this child, beyond the
fact that he will persist in his errors, will also be
stymied in his natural development. The child
who wants to do something by himself is completely cooperative and animated. If we see that
he is struggling, we immediately step in to help
him finish the task he started.

Perhaps the voice of temptation sounds like
this: "You want to wash yourself and dress yourself, but don't let it bother you; I am here and
can do everything your heart desires." The child,
whom we have robbed of his own will, becomes
difficult; we take this misbehavior into account
and believe that by doing things for him we will
do him some good.

We must think of what happens to the child

who, for the first few years of his life, is closed up in a house where there is nothing but things that he must neither break nor soil, where he cannot exercise mastery over himself or learn the use of the common objects of daily life. He will be deprived of much necessary experience and his life will always manifest this lack.

There are also children whom no one ever succeeds in handling well. They are always restless and sullen, they never want to wash, and their parents leave them alone and never interfere. Everybody says that such parents are good and patient for putting up with such children every day. But is this really being good? What an erroneous idea of goodness!

Real goodness does not consist of putting up with every kind of aberration, but of seeking the means to avoid it; it consists of every act that extends to the child the possibility of living naturally. It consists of giving the child what he needs to live; in understanding that he is an impoverished little creature, that he has nothing and that he must be given that which he needs. This is goodness and compassion.

When we watch a child in an environment that is his and that evokes response in him, we see that he works by himself toward his own self-perfection. The right way is not only indicated by the objects he picks up, but by the

possibility of his recognizing his own errors by
means of these objects.

And what should we do?

Nothing.

We have exerted the effort to get him the
things that he needs. Now we must learn to take
ourselves in hand and watch from the sidelines,
following him at a distance, neither tiring him
with our intervention nor abandoning him. He is
always tranquil and self-sufficient while he is
occupied with something that is very important
to him. What remains for us to do other than to
observe? It was for this reason I created a school
in which the children spontaneously developed
their own activities while the teacher was rele-
gated to the role of observer, exactly the opposite
of the ordinary school, where the teacher assumes the active role while the children remain
passive. The more the children progress, the
more the teacher must be limited to observation.

Out of this came a charming episode from
one of our schools. The janitor forgot to unlock
the door of the school and the children were very
unhappy because they could not get in. Finally,
the teacher said, "You children can get in through
the windows, but I can't." So the children went
in through the window and the teacher contented
herself with watching from outside.

A felicitous environment that guides the
children and offers them the means to exercise

their own faculties permits the teacher to absent herself temporarily. The creation of such an environment is already the realization of great progress.

9
THE
CHILD
IN THE FAMILY

We have seen so far that most childhood education is based upon false ideas and erroneous preconceptions, although today there are some attempts being made to promulgate rather more positive ideas based on immediate observation. Considering the success reported in the cases of methods based on observation in every area, it seems obvious that the direction of pedagogy will change. Modern educational methods, based on the necessity to observe the child before hazarding an approach, will finally penetrate the family too and create there not only a new child, but a new mother and father.

Until now, the principal training parents gave their children consisted of correcting their inadequacies, teaching them that which appeared to be good and right, although not so much by example as with moral precept and admonition— if these did not suffice, then with shouts and blows. Indeed, it was a peace-loving society in which no one had more right to resort to physical punishment as a means of education than the family.

But such a right burdened parents with two responsibilities: they represented to defenseless children power and intransigent authority, and further, they were obliged to function continually as examples. Parents understand full well their role in determining how their children will turn out, or, as the popular saying has it: the hand that rocks the cradle rules the world. Yet a mother who knows that in her own childhood only by practice and patience did she succeed in learning the simplest task will still be unable to apply this action to the education of her own children. A father who learned so much from his youth will take no pains to reflect upon how to form a child's character, nor will he observe the child with any care. As a result, the parents' immense responsibility is often abandoned, whether carelessly or through the best will in the world, or even because the experiences of the past lack vividness because they were empty to begin with.

It is, of course, difficult suddenly to become models of perfection worthy of children's imitation. At any rate, until the family grew with the arrival of a new, innocent life, the parents competed in pointing out each other's defects. Suddenly they are faced with a new duty: that of being perfect. To them falls the task of educating their children, of correcting defects, and improving with punishments and, above all, through the shining example of their own perfection. Thus a situation is created that we cannot discuss minutely here because of the difficulties and contradictions of daily life.

Let us look at the problem of lying.

One of the most important tasks of the good mother is to inculcate in her child the habit of telling the truth. One mother of my acquaintance was teaching her little girl that she must never lie by depicting the baseness of lying. At the same time she was praising the courage and firmness of character of those ready to sacrifice everything to a good cause, even to committing an action thoroughly blameworthy. She strove to make the child understand that from a single lie came a long series of wrong acts, which led to all that is bad in the world and justified the proverb: the liar robs minds. She emphasized above all the duty of the rich and of people of good family to maintain their dignity and create good examples for the poor, who have no other means of a good education.

But one day this lady received an invitation to a concert over the telephone. Speaking loudly, she said, "What a shame! I really can't go out; I have a dreadful headache." She had scarcely finished speaking when she heard a shriek from the next room; she ran in and found her little girl had thrown herself upon the floor, her face hidden in her hands. "What happened to you, darling?" "Mamma told a lie!" wept the child.

Her faith was destroyed and a wall rose between the mother and child. Her social ideas were confused, their sacredness to the child profaned. The mother who had taken such pains to instill habits of truth in her child had not thought of the lies she was in the habit of telling every day.

Often those adults who work tirelessly to encourage the habit of truth in the child surround him with the kind of falseness that cannot even be reckoned as a "little lie" but is premeditated and has as its end the deception of the child. In respect to this let me relate an anecdote about Christmas and Santa Claus. One day, a mother who resented painfully being a party to this particular deception confessed it to her little girl, who was so disappointed that she had been deceived that she was depressed for a week. Her mother wept when she recounted this little drama to me.

But the situation is not always this serious. Another made the same confession to her little boy. He started to laugh and said, "Oh, Mamma! I've known for a long time that Santa Claus doesn't exist!" "But why didn't you ever tell me?" "Because it always made you so happy." The roles are often reversed. Children, who are the most acute observers, have pity on their parents and agree with them in order to please them.

Many parents believe that their children should submit to order without any discussion and, at the same time, would have their children love them with all their hearts. Here, too, the child is often the teacher of the parent, for his thoughts are pure and his sense of justice unbelievable.

One evening, a good mother wanted her child to go to bed. The child begged to be allowed to finish some work he had started, but his mother would not give in. The child ended up by going to bed but later got up again in order to finish what he had been doing. His mother found him at it and scolded him bitterly for having tried to deceive her. "I didn't deceive you," the child responded. "I told you before that I wanted to finish this." To stop the discussion, his mother ordered him to apologize. But the little boy per-

sisted in arguing about the word *deceive*, as he
had persisted before in not leaving his work; he
continued to explain that he had deceived no one
and therefore he failed to see why he should
apologize. "Very well," said his mother, "I see
that you don't love me!" "But, Mamma," replied
the child, "I love you very much, but why
should I apologize when I am right!" It would
seem that the child had spoken like an adult and
the mother like a child.

Here is another example dealing with a father who was pastor of a Protestant church and
whose young daughter assisted him every Sunday. One Sunday, the pastor preached about the
compassion of Jesus and said that all men are
brothers, that the poor and the afflicted remember Jesus and that we must love them if we want
eternal salvation. The little girl left the church
deeply moved, and, on the way home, met a
poor little girl, covered with sores, who was begging for money. The girl ran to her and hugged
and kissed her with affection. Her parents, hor-
rified, pulled their little girl, so clean and well
dressed, hurriedly away and scolded her well for
her behavior. When they reached home, they
scrubbed her with hot water and changed her
clothes. From that time on, the little girl listened
to her father's sermons with the same indifference she manifested toward other tales that had
no effect upon her life.

As in these anecdotes, there are an infinite number of other conflicts generated out of the poor rapport between parents and their offspring, or actually, between adults and children.

Our pretensions and our insufficiencies put us in a false position as far as our children are concerned and carry us continually to those conflicts that ultimately become actual battles between parents and children. An abyss opens between us and our children, and no one can bridge it. Although in battle the stronger usually wins, often the adult does not succeed in dominating his little rival and finally has recourse to persuasive methods exactly because he is wrong. In these cases, the parents tend to resolve ugly situations in an authoritarian manner: they oblige their children to obedience, maintaining a posture of perfection. Having attained the victory, they render it valid by ordering their children to be silent, and thus "peace" is assured! In the meantime, the children lose faith in their parents and all the spontaneity and confidence in the relationship dies.

The child's deepest and most compelling necessities are in this way unfulfilled. As a result, he will manifest certain characteristic reactions, or, from his adaptation to the unjust behavior of the adult, he conceals certain physical tensions that can degenerate sometimes into pathological conditions. This kind of damage is so common that it can be considered characteristic of the child, while it is actually a defense mechanism, such as shyness, or willful lying to conceal some bit of misbehavior. Fear, too, like lying, arises from this passive submission, although it is somewhat more serious because it generates confused imaginings and feelings. Confusion appears in children who lack any opportunity for a tranquil inner development. To these ills we must add that of passive imitativeness. This is an entranceway for moral infection rather than a means of self-perfection and evolution; we do not progress through watching others since progress is uniquely our own work. Those desires that are repressed in the child lay hidden, like putrifying matter in a stagnant pool, and the child is never capable of appraising them at their true worth. Because they have never been realized, because they cannot be restrained since he has never had the opportunity to master them, because they are always present, they attract him little by little and seduce him through his secretive interest.

Because the adult suffocates the child's natural impulse to act, he impedes the child's ability to live, to do anything useful, to exert great energy; in a word, he becomes an obstacle in the way of the child's developing according to his own natural laws. As a consequence, the child travels the wrong road and he turns to a thousand useless objects, toys, and such frivolities, which serve no purpose whatsoever. A paralyzed unconscious has reduced his being, which should be capable of surmounting every obstacle, to decay in resigned inertia and sloth.

Such a child has had the wings of his childhood and the healthy impulse toward activity clipped. His imagination does not close upon lively things that might interest him, but is erring and without feeling, seeking vainly in the external world for a natural point of contact. Thus is born in the child, precisely because reality in all its forms is hidden from him, a sickly and fantastical form of life that withdraws completely into unreality.

But the little spirit battles and defends itself constantly. As with all impotent creatures, this opposition manifests itself in nervous fits, willfulness, anger, tears and tantrums. The child involves himself in the kind of mischievousness—for the most part, another aspect of angry and premeditated rebellion—that consumes not the right energy but other kinds, which he dissipates through malignity and irritating little acts that can only be dreamed up by an unoccupied, lazy imagination.

Further, it happens that these little rebels, who are the desperation of their teachers or anyone who has to deal with them, find among the other children imitators and little followers. Certainly an adult would not behave differently toward an enemy who, penetrating the sanctuaries and daring to lay down laws, came to crush the will of the conquered and unarmed.

The child's nervous system suffers in this conflict, and today doctors are beginning to understand that the immediate causes of many emotional maladies is repression during infancy. Often during infancy there appear such dangerous symptoms as insomnia, nightmares, digestive disturbances and stammering, and all these have a single cause.

Parents honestly do all that is possible to cure the emotional illnesses of their children and they strive to meliorate defects of character. They exhaust themselves curing ills they themselves have caused and that will persist into maturity. All this is poured into that oppression which, redressed as love, denies all the real needs of the child.

We must free the child's oppressed spirit! Then, as if by magic, all the ills caused by oppression will disappear, and those that remain will be purely constitutional.

Imperfect humanity always feels the need of an authority that will teach the truth and point out the right road from which one must never stray.

But now we must consider another aspect of the problem. Although young parents are to liberate the imprisoned spirits of their children, who are somewhat more innocent and pure, they ought not take the idea of educational freedom to mean that they ought never correct defects in general. Were they to think so, they would expose the child to the many consequences of such neglect, largely the danger of emotional ills. I am not setting down new principles here, but simply drawing other conclusions. Before I apply these, however, we must think of what actually happens to the child and what we must do by way of satisfying him. But to achieve this end, it is necessary to prepare the parents.

Now, as ever, almost all mothers are well versed in the kind of physical care necessary for the growth of their children and they know the rules of proper diet, proper adjustment to temperature and the advantages of play in the fresh air that increases the oxygen supply to the lungs. The child is not merely a little animal to feed, but from the time of his birth, a creature with a spirit. If we must look after his welfare, then it is not enough to content ourselves with his physical needs: we must open the way for his spiritual development. We must, from the very first day, respect the impulses of his spirit and know how to support them.

There are clear rules to follow for physical hygiene, but the rules for spiritual hygiene extend into a larger realm and are yet to be understood. The child not only feels the need for food. His joy at achieving certain given movements with which no one interferes is for us a sign of his vast inner necessities. Instead of inhibiting his activity, we must create the means for him to develop it.

Most modern toys do not offer the spiritual stimulation that is relevant to the child and I believe that they will ultimately be withdrawn from the market. Let us look at the changes of the past few years. Toys have grown increasingly larger. The doll has become so big that it is almost as tall as the little girl, and, correspondingly, so has everything else that pertains to the doll: the bed, the dresser, the stove and so forth.

But the little girl is not pleased by this.

If the toys continue to be made larger, the little girl becomes the rival of her doll, and will want for herself the little bed and the chairs. She will have then reached the heights of happiness, but the doll will be discarded. The little girl will have found an environment for herself and will use for herself with great joy all those things that were destined for her doll. All those lovely, useful things will procure for her a new life—a real life—the only life that can make her happy and help her to grow in a natural way.

We must give the child an environment that he can utilize by himself: a little washstand of his own, some small chairs, a bureau with drawers

he can open, objects of common use that he can
operate, a small bed in which he can sleep at
night under an attractive blanket he can fold and
spread by himself. We must give him an environment in which he can live and play; then we will
see him work all day with his hands and wait
impatiently to undress by himself and lay himself
down on his own bed. He will dust the furniture,
put it in order, take care to eat well, dress by
himself, be gracious and tranquil, without tears,
without tantrums, without naughtiness—affectionate and obedient.

The new education prepares an adaptive
environment for the child and recognizes in general that he loves work and order for themselves.
It also provides the necessary opportunity to observe him and recognizes the particular exigencies of his spirit as it begins to unfold. The new
way is the way of the spirit; it does not ignore
that which is already known about bodily health,
but appropriates that knowledge and utilizes it to
make new progress. Certainly the psychological
aspect of existence is the most important for us;
this is the basis of the new education.

Now let me enumerate the principles that
will help the mother find the best way for her
child.

The most important is to respect all the
reasonable forms of activity in which the child
engages and to try to understand them.

We tend to ignore those usual expressions of life that indicate the child's inner powers and that impel him to develop his energies in all areas. When we speak of childrens' activities, we think of something particular that we have observed, perhaps because it has jolted our usual inattention. Perhaps we could also deal with some naughty reaction or some psychic deviation produced by an explosion of energy too long repressed. On the contrary, the real signs of children's activity are not very easy to find. We must believe in all the good that lies hidden in the child and prepare ourselves to recognize it with loving concern; only in this fashion will we gradually begin to assess the child correctly. Parents must begin to prepare themselves in this way if they want to arrive at a reasonable understanding of the natural manifestations of children.

At any rate, here are some observations on the child in the family.

First, let me talk about a three-month-old girl, a tiny being on the threshold of life. I observed a little girl in the process of discovering her hands. She made every effort to observe them better, but her arms were too short, and in order to see her hands, she had to move her eyes with great effort. There was a great deal to see around her, but only her hands interested her. Her efforts were an instinctual expression, one that sacrificed comfort itself in order to attain an inner satisfaction.

Later on, I gave this little girl something to hold and touch, but she did so indifferently; apparently it did not interest her. She opened her little hand and let it fall without the slightest notice. From then on, her face took on the brightest expression every time she tried to grasp something, near her or not, with or without success. She kept looking questioningly at her hands, as if to say, "How is it sometimes I succeed in holding something and sometimes I don't?" Evidently, the problem of using her hands had attracted her attention. When she was six months old, I gave her a rattle with a silver bell. I put it in her hand and helped her to shake it to sound the bell. After a few minutes, she dropped it; I picked it up and gave it to her again, and so it went several times over.

It seemed as if the child intentionally dropped the rattle in order to have it returned to her immediately afterward. One day, while she was holding it, instead of completely opening her hand as usual, she lifted first one finger, then another and another and finally the last, and the rattle fell to the floor. The baby looked intently at her fingers. She repeated the movements, continuing to watch her fingers. Clearly, what interested her was not the rattle but the game, the function of those fingers that knew how to hold

119

the object, and this observation made her happy. Earlier the child had forced her eyes into an uncomfortable position in order to look at her hands, and now she was studying their function. Her wise mother limited herself to recovering the rattle; thus she was taking part in her little daughter's activity and understanding the great importance that lay in the repetition of the game.

This incident illustrates the simplest needs of the child at the earliest stage of his life. But had that little girl not been well observed, perhaps her hands might have been covered, perversely impeding her desire to watch them, or perhaps her parents might have taken away the rattle because they saw that she kept dropping it on the floor, and all I have recounted would have passed unobserved. The best and most natural means for developing this little girl's intellectual powers would have been repressed. Instead of enjoying her discovery, the child would have burst into tears, seemingly without reason, and from her infancy on, the wall of misunderstanding would have been begun between us and this little spirit.

Perhaps many doubt that an inner life exists in the very young child. Certainly, these people must learn to understand the special language of the spirit if they would understand the needs of these tiny beings and be persuaded of the importance of these needs for the life that is developing. Respect for the liberty of the child consists of helping these powers to grow.

Here is another case. A boy of about a year old was looking one day at some drawings his mother had made for him before he was born. The boy kissed the pictures of children and was especially attracted to those of the smallest children. He could also distinguish the pictures of flowers and put his nose against the paper as if he were smelling them. It was clear that the child knew how to behave with both children and flowers. Some of the people present thought the child quite charming and began to laugh, picking up a quantity of objects as if to kiss and smell them, laughing all the while, as if such actions had no other significance than the comic. They offered the child crayons to smell and cushions to kiss, but he became thoroughly confused, and the bright, intelligent expression that had tranfigured his face earlier disappeared. Earlier, he had been completely happy because he had known how to distinguish things in the drawings and how to behave toward each; it was a new, important acquisition of his intelligence, this reasonable occupation that had made him so happy. But he had not the inner strength to defend himself against the brutal intervention of adults. He ended up smelling and kissing everything indiscriminately, laughing as those around him laughed, and for him the way to independent development was barred.

How often do we do something like this to our children without knowing it! We suffocate their natural instincts and often provoke the desperate anxiety that finally comes to those tears "without cause," the tears of those children about whom, blindly, we have not cared, as we have failed to notice the happy smile that comes with the satisfaction of a spiritual necessity. And this happens at the very beginning of life, when the impressions are particularly delicate and when the child has just begun to feel the first promptings of the human spirit. From this moment, the battle has begun between the child and the adult.

If we cradle the child, he sleeps. We do not hate the spirit that cries for help!

If, however, the child is active, we see immediately that he requires rather less sleep. His eyes are bright and intelligent and manifest the first signs of sociability. He wants help and will turn to anyone who will give it to him. People often say that the little child does not love his mother as much as the breast that nurtures him, just as he will later love anyone who will give him goodies. No: already in those first steps of life he will love anyone who will help him to perfect his spirit.

It is manifest that children seek the company of adults and try in every way to take part in their lives. The child is completely satisfied only when he sits at the table with the family or warms himself before the fire with them.

Those human voices that speak of peace and tranquility surely make the most beautiful music. Nature offers us this means to learn to speak.

The second principle is this: *We must support as much as possible the child's desires for activity; not wait on him, but educate him to be independent.*

Until now, the first words and the first steps always served as visible and almost symbolic milestones of childhood development and were the earliest proofs of progress. The first word indicated the development of language; the first step attested to the ability to stand upright and walk. These were, therefore, the most important events in a family, and the wise and intelligent mother made a note of when they occurred.

But walking and speaking are rather difficult accomplishments. It requires a great deal of effort before the child succeeds in keeping that tiny body with the oversized head in balance and in standing up on those short, little legs. Even that first word is a rather complex means of expression. Certainly these two conquests cannot be the first in the child's life. His intellect and his sense of balance have already come a long way, and the word and the step are nothing but the most apparent stages; but the road that has already been traversed in order to arrive at these two conquests merits all our attention.

It is true that the child develops naturally, but it is precisely because of this that he must get a great deal of exercise. If he lacks exercise, his intelligence remains on a lower level; I would almost say that there seems to be a kind of arresting of the development of those children who from the time they were infants were supported and guided.

Those who do not care about little children are those who brutally shove the cereal spoon into the child's mouth from the very first meals after nursing. If, instead, one sits with the child at his little table and allows enough time for eating, he will see immediately that a little hand will reach out for the spoon to carry it to the mouth.

This is a great achievement for a mother, and it requires great love and patience. She must simultaneously feed the body and the spirit, but the spirit takes precedence. She may even have some notions—certainly the most praiseworthy—concerning cleanliness, but in this instance they are quite secondary; the child who has just begun to eat by himself will not know how to do it and as a consequence will get himself filthy. One must simply sacrifice cleanliness to the justifiable impulse to act; in the course of his development, the child will perfect his movements and learn to eat without dirtying himself. Cleanliness achieved in this fashion represents real progress, a triumph for the child's spirit.

The capacity of the child's will is demonstrated in the quantity of meaningful movements he can continually achieve. Even before he speaks, indeed, even before he walks— somewhere near the end of his first year of life— he begins to act as if he were obeying an inner voice. He will try to eat using a spoon in the conventional manner, but he will not succeed in carrying the food he wants to his mouth; he is hungry, but he rejects any assistance. Only after he has satisfied his own needs to act will he accept the help of his mother. He may be horribly dirty but his face shines with happiness and intelligence. Now, because his own energies are satisfied, he eats everything happily. And we see, and marvel, that a child educated in this fashion succeeds in serving himself and feeding himself by the end of his first year. He does not yet know how to talk, but he understands perfectly well everything that is said to him and seeks to respond to our words with actions.

These natural actions of the child give the impression of a precocious intelligence. We tell him, "Wash your hands!" and he obeys. The same happens when we ask him to pick his things up off the floor or to wipe them off—he executes everything with zeal.

One day I was in the country in the company of a little boy about one year old who had just learned to walk, and we were on a rocky pathway. My first impulse was to take him by the hand, but then I restrained myself and sought to guide him with words: "Walk on that side!" and "Watch, there is a rock! Be careful here!" He listened with a kind of friendly seriousness and obeyed. He neither fell nor did poorly. I guided him step by step, murmuring softly, and he listened attentively and enjoyed taking part in this meaningful activity of understanding my words and responding with his own actions. To guide a child in this fashion—that is the real job of the mother.

Real help must not be offered for useless or arbitrary things; it must correspond to the efforts of the child's spirit. It must be predicated upon an understanding of the child's nature and respect for his instinctive activity.

The third principle is that we must be most watchful in our relationships with children because they are quite sensitive—more than we know—to external influences.

If we have neither sufficient experience nor love to enable us to distinguish the fine and delicate expressions of the child's life, if we do not know how to respect them, then we perceive them only when they are manifested violently. At this point, our help comes too late. For the most part, we see these expressions only when we have not satisfied some need of the child and he bursts into tears; then we hasten to console him.

Some parents, however, hold different pedagogical principles; they are not bothered by the tears of their children because they know by experience that these children will start to cry and then quiet down by themselves. If they do try to console the children—so they say—the children will be spoiled and will end up habitually using tears to attract attention, while the parents will become the slaves of spoiled children.

I must respond that the tears that are apparently without reason begin before the child has become used to our caresses. Tears are the index of a real anguish that he suffers. The child needs rest and a peaceful sameness in order to construct his inner life; yet, instead, we disturb him with our continual, brutal interruptions. We hurl a quantity of disordered impressions at him that are often sustained with such rapidity that he has no time to absorb them. Then the child cries in the same way he would if he were hungry or had eaten too much and was feeling the first signs of digestive disturbance.

We ought to console the child as much as we let him dry his tears by himself, for at any rate we have neglected what he really needs. The essential cause of these tears escapes us because it is too subtle, yet in this lies the explanation of everything.

Helen was a little girl not yet one year old and often used the Catalan word *pupa* for *bad*. Furthermore, she never cried without a clear reason. We noticed that she said *pupa* whenever she experienced something unpleasant: if she hit a hard object, felt cold, touched marble or passed her hand over a rough surface. It was clear she wanted to understand what was around her. People responded to her with a sympathetic word or kissed the tiny finger she offered to show where she had been hurt. She would observe attentively what one did with her and, immediately consoled, would say, "Pupa no!" that is, "I feel better, you don't have to console me anymore." In this fashion, she was observing her own impressions and those of the people around her. She was not a spoiled child, because no one showered her with caresses or consoled her longer than was necessary. But by dealing directly with her impressions, we helped her to clarify her observations and develop her social instincts; thus, we were serving to control and support her first experiences in life. The fine and ingenuous sensitivity of her nature was developing without handicaps. We never said to her, "It's nothing," when she said she had experienced something unpleasant. We accepted her unpleasant experience and sought to console her tenderly without placing undue emphasis on what had happened.

To say to a child who has experienced something unpleasant, "It's nothing!" serves to confuse him because it negates an impression of his own for which he sought confirmation. Our participation, on the other hand, gives him the courage to encounter other experiences and, at the same time, shows him how to relate to them. They must not be denied, or talked about too much, or analyzed too deeply! A tender and affectionate word is the only consoling response. Having had this, the child can continue his observations and experiences by himself, freely, and his physical development will benefit greatly.

Little Helen was not a whiner. If something bad happened to her, she repeated the word pupa and wanted to be consoled, but she almost never cried. Once when she was ill, she continually said to her mother, "Pupa, no!" as if to console herself. Her capacity to endure physical discomfort was quite remarkable for her age; she had a well-ordered comprehension of sensation and bore her little ailments like an adult.

Often children weep heartbrokenly if they see someone else suffer. Both little Helen and little Lawrence were quite sensitive in this respect. If someone pretended to strike their nurse, or if their father pretended to beat one of their friends, they would burst into tears. If someone complained or cried for any reason, the little girl would immediately run over and kiss him tenderly. But right after that she would say with a certain assurance, "Pupa, no!" meaning "No, everything is all right and let's not talk about it anymore!" She did not yet know how to speak, but what clarity and firmness she possessed! Lawrence, however, would go further; he would courageously reprove his father. If his father made some impetuous movement, or pushed his little boy, Lawrence would not cry, but would stand in front of him, looking at him with great seriousness, and say in reproving tone, "Daddy, Daddy!" implying, "You must not do that to me!"

One day Lawrence was in his bed and wanted to sleep; his father was in a nearby room speaking loudly with another person. Lawrence sat up in his bed and shouted, "Daddy!" His father, after the admonition, lowered his voice; Lawrence, satisfied, stretched himself out again and fell asleep. I remember another little episode when Helen was a bit older, about three years old. Her aunt was showing her the coloring sets that are part of my educational materials. One of the sets fell to the floor and broke, and her aunt took advantage of the occasion to say, "Look, you must be very careful with these sets." "Then pay attention," said Helen, "and don't drop them!" This is the way it is; they judge and reprove adults, and only when adults interfere for the best reason will their sense of justice be satisfied.

It is not absolutely necessary that we appear perfect in the eyes of children; rather, it is necessary that we recognize our defects and patiently accept the children's just observations. Recognizing this principle, we can excuse ourselves before children when we have done something unjust.

One day Helen's aunt said to her, "Sweetheart, I was very rude to you this morning, and you didn't deserve it; I was in a terrible mood!" "But, Auntie dear," said the little girl, hugging her, "you know I love you very very much!"

It is not our duty to be examples of perfection for the child, for in their eyes we will always have our defects, but often they see these more clearly than we do and can help us to recognize and correct them.

To follow attentively all the spiritual expressions of a child is to free him so he can manifest his needs and thereby guarantee for himself all the external means for his progress. This is the premise for his freedom and harmonious development and the germination of his energies.

10
THE
NEW
TEACHER

The basis for our educational system lies in the use of various stimuli to awaken a sense of security in the child. It is, moreover, not necessary to assign absolute values to these stimuli. Their greater or lesser efficacy depends upon the teacher and how she presents the educational materials to the child. Because of this, she must know how to render the material attractive to the child so that it will be most effective, although the degree of effectiveness can only be determined by the teacher herself and by her method of presentation. Let us look at the lessons, or the teaching itself, that special ability to present materials to a child and instruct him in their use.

Those who study our method are greatly occupied with everything regarding the teaching and find it interesting to make the comparison between the lessons given in our schools and those in others where the teaching is traditional.

In our kind of teaching, the essential part of the activity is initiated by the child. As soon as the child has reached the age when he is capable of meaningful action, he is in a position to continue his education on his own, repeating voluntarily those physical exercises that engage the reasoning process. He accomplishes in this fashion a work that is perfectly independent, in which he involves himself and in which the teacher does not interfere. Her job is limited to offering the materials and suffices if she demonstrates their use; after that, she leaves the child with his work. Our goal is not so much the imparting of knowledge as the unveiling and developing of spiritual energy.

The number of such lessons must be rather high, for the child tends to ignore almost all the things that surround him, and he cannot guess their uses himself. For this reason, the teacher stands ready to demonstrate. Many teachers have asked me if it is enough to offer the materials in a gentle and encouraging fashion. It is actually not enough, because the manner of use is most

important. Consider, for example, eating uten-
sils. We all know very well how to use them, but
if an Oriental who did not know how to use them
saw them on a table, he would be amused and
would pass them from one hand to the other
since he would never have seen anyone using
them.

Therefore, the teacher works out lessons continually—arranging cubes one on top of the other according to their sizes, building a kind of
tower that she later demolishes, removing cylinders from the blocks, mixing them up and leaving
them to be put back together according to size,
or setting a game out on the floor. These lessons
may appear strange, because they are carried out
in almost complete silence, while one thinks in
general that a lesson signifies an oral recitation,
almost a tiny lecture. Yet his wordless instruction
is an actual "lesson." It shows the child how to
sit, how to stand, how to carry a little table or a
tray with glasses of water, how to move easily
and surely. Are these not, after all, lessons? Even
silence is a lesson. With this kind of exercise we
teach the child to sit quietly, and we accustom
him to maintaining this position until a soft voice
calls his name. We direct his attention to the
movements of his body and encourage him to
learn to control them perfectly. The teacher never encourages this tranquility with words, but
with her own quiet sureness. Thus, we can say

that our own "tranquility lessons" are symbolic of our method. We teach everything in this fashion, even those things that most people believe cannot be understood without words.

In our schools the environment itself teaches the children. The teacher only puts the child in direct contact with the environment, showing him how to use various things. But this never succeeds in other methods. One hears only commands: "Be quiet!" "Stop wiggling!" And these are supposed to be the words of education! We, on the other hand, do not believe in the educative power of words and commands alone, but seek cautiously, and almost without the child's knowing it, to guide his natural activity. It is he who demonstrates the success of our method, acquiring new capacities and perfecting them by assiduous exercise on his own initiative. But obeying a command presupposes an already formed personality. In other words, the child ought already to have acquired the faculty to react as we wish because obedience must be won by his exercising it and cannot be attained solely on command. How often does one hear a piano teacher say, "Hold your fingers better!" without showing the pupil how to hold them! The pupil again puts his fingers in a bad position, the teacher repeats her observation and the pupil continues to hold his fingers badly.

A command must be preceded by something that is essential: a certain order must have been achieved in the course of the development of the child's spirit that makes it possible for the child to submit to the adult and to obey him. The child achieves this order by himself and guards it carefully. All oral instruction should come relatively late in the course of instruction, since before the child has attained a state of internal order it is impossible to think of guiding him. Of course the word too must be taught, but the child's vocabulary and his way of using it should be taken into account.

Often inexperienced teachers place great importance on teaching and believe they have done everything necessary when they have demonstrated the use of the materials in a meaningful way. In reality, they are far from the truth because the job of the teacher is rather more important than that. To her falls the task of guiding the development of the child's spirit, and therefore her observations of the child are not limited solely to understanding him. All her observations must emerge at the end—and this is their only justification—in her ability to help the child.

The task of the new teacher is a hard one, and I try to remember every principle that can help her. Before everything, she must know how to recognize the polarizing of attention. When the child is attentive to his great work, she must respect the fact and not disturb him with either

praise or correction. A few teachers understand
this principle only imperfectly; they distribute
the materials, retire and maintain silence whatever happens. Consequently, there is great disorder
in the class. The respect for the child's activity,
which we call nonintervention, is justifiable only
when something substantial has already inter-
vened in his life—that is, when he has acquired
the ability to direct all his attention on something
and dedicate himself to it, when he has revealed
all his interest (not just his curiosity). The respect
is not justified when the child's good energies are
dispersed in disorder. One time I saw an entire
class of disorganized children who were using the
materials completely wrongly. The teacher drift-
ed about in the class, silent as the Sphinx. I
asked her if it would not be better if the children
went out to play. Then I passed by one child
whispering quietly into the ear of another. "What
are you doing?" I asked him. "I'm speaking
softly so as not to disturb him."

This teacher was committing a grave error:
she feared disturbing their disorder, instead of
attempting to establish the order that favors individual work by the children.

One time a teacher made this observation to
me: "You want us to respect the child's concentration as much as we would that of a scientist or
an artist, but then why do you say that we
should intervene if the children are amusing

themselves with the educational material rather than working?" "That's true," I said, "I respect the intellectual activity of the child as much as the inspiration of the artist; however, this respect holds the inspiration in higher regard than the artist's. If, for example, I enter his studio and find him intent upon smoking or playing cards, certainly I will not hesitate to disturb him and will speak to him, 'Well, my friend, what is keeping you so busy?' That kind of occupation only absorbs him a little! 'Put down your pipe and let's take a walk and enjoy the sun!' "

Our method certainly does not encourage respect for defects or superficiality. It is essentially based on the ability to recognize the difference among the physical states of the child, encouraging those conducive to his spiritual health (these we can call the good), and discouraging the others, which are neither constructive nor formative and lead to the destruction of his development and the useless scattering of his energies (we call these states evil).

We must take this distinction to heart, not only as teachers but also as mothers.

The teacher can address the pupil energetically and severely and thus jolt him out of his behavior, but those who know their jobs well have means more effective than coercion for recalling the pupil to order. Without doubt this requires constant surveillance and continual work; the teacher must watch over and carefully arrange the surroundings. How much simpler this is than commanding and admonishing! Yet, on the other hand, it is not an easy task and requires great love and insight.

The teacher must occupy herself with the child's environment in the same way that a wife cares for her husband's home by making it attractive and pleasant. But that is not enough; she must know what is happening with the child and she must set with her own hands the cradle of the intellect that is forming. Working and observing, the teacher will end with a clear vision of her task. The child's order and disorder, the successes he attains, depend often on one's ability to observe the least particulars, because only through doing will the result be satisfactory.

Let me give an example to demonstrate how an error, apparently insignificant, gave rise to certain remote consequences. Imagine a completely furnished house. If the tenants use the washbasins for coal storage they certainly cannot wash themselves and will damage the house and the furnishings. They cannot use the hygienic advantages that were at their disposal and therefore remain in their miserable condition, all because of an apparently tiny error. Where they had expected great results, they got nothing; they created disorder instead of order.

The teacher's ability rests on the thoughtful

application of the bases of our method. If she can identify these, she will find the help necessary to combat little difficulties, and she will achieve great results.

The way is the same for every kind of perfection, even moral perfection. The knowledge of how to conquer even a little sin, however pardonable, is not necessarily the achievement of perfection, but the spirit that knows how to free itself from weakness can rise up and, while overcoming its defects, make it possible for the force of good to shape its energies. It is in this fashion that the little difficulties are scattered.

We must help the child to liberate himself from his defects without making him feel his weakness.

11
THE
ADULT
AND THE CHILD

Education today is considered not only a technological science but a most important field of study in the larger area of the social sciences. In fact, it is clear that humanity progresses not only by means of those sciences that transform the external environment but, more immediately, through that science addressed directly to the needs of man in development: to the child. For this reason, not only scientists and educators are interested in the findings related to the field of education, but parents and the general public as well. Everyone knows the two principles of modern pedagogy. The first is to study and form individuality: to know every child as himself and

to reach him through his own particular character traits. The second principle concerns the
necessity to free the child.

It is well known that the realization of the
goals of modern pedagogy has encountered obstacles difficult to overcome, and yet pedagogical
science has already solved an enormous number
of problems. Indeed, the word "problem" is
characteristic of this area of research—people
speak of the "school problem," of the "problem
of freedom," the "problem of interest and energy," and so forth, while in other scientific fields,
practitioners use the word "law"—the "law of
light diffusion," the "law of gravity," and so on.
In the sciences, generally, the problems occur in
obscure and peripheral areas; the heart of science
consists in discovery and problem solving. On the
other hand, in the area of experimental modern
pedagogy, it would appear that to leave the
field of significant problems is to leave the
realm of science altogether, for all that is scientific about solving insignificant problems is the
manner of research and observation. Whoever
would say, "I have resolved all the problems of
pedagogy, I have made discoveries about the
human spirit, I have put education on a sure and
simple level," would not be taken at all seriously
by scientists. Indeed, there exist sharp contrasts
between the freedom of the scholar and the
necessity that he work within disciplinary lines or

within the culture; between individual development and social pressure, for in human society
there are inevitable restraints upon the individual
who must adapt not only to the often hard necessities of the unanticipated, but also to the moral
limitations that shore up the stability of the civil
community. Therefore he must come to sacrifice,
to a greater or lesser degree, his individuality.
Applying this to the child, it seems inevitable
that he must suffer under his scholastic obliga-
tions, however desirable it would be that he enjoy them; he must strive but not exhaust himself.
It is imperative that he obey, yet desirable that
he be free. It is the confrontation between these
ideals and the realities that generates the problems of education. The attempts of the scientists
end up sounding like the laments of adults con-
templating the fate of children. In fact, all the
reforms of the modern school are designed to
alleviate inevitable evils—for example, the revi-
sion in the lessons and the program in general,
the obligatory rest period and physical exercise.
These remedies in the final analysis have had
detrimental effects upon cultural progress.

At any rate, the solutions to such problems
cannot be compromise. We must have actual
reform; we must trace new paths for education,
which up to now has been negotiating a cul-de-
sac.

Educational science has not found a felicitous method, while in other scientific areas one finds brilliant discoveries, useful for human life. In our area, everything has been limited to the study of external phenomena. To borrow medical terminology, we might say that it was an attempt to cure the symptoms without seeking the essential but obscure cause.

In medicine, it is possible to identify the most diverse symptoms as having arisen from a central cause capable of generating innumerable external signs that can only be vainly dealt with singly. For example, a functional disorder of the heart can generate different symptoms in all the organs, and it would be vain to try to cure one of these symptoms without trying to re-establish a normal condition of the heart—the symptoms would simply reappear immediately. Another example might be the manner in which neurosis is dealt with in psychoanalysis: the analyst finds himself in the presence of a complicated interplay of feelings and ideas resulting in a veritable chaos of incomprehensible phenomena, and he must reconstruct the successive stages back to the single cause buried in the subconscious. When this cause is revealed, everything becomes meaningful, and the symptoms either disappear or are rendered innocuous.

The problems of education that I have been discussing can be analogized to the external symptom, in itself irreducible, which develops

from an obscure central cause buried, one might
say, in the social subconscious of mankind. My
pedagogical method has remained outside the
"symptomatic procedure" of existing education
and has followed the road that promised to reveal the central cause of all the effects previously
thought to be irreducible. This cause has been
conquered, and the problems have disappeared.

Now we can see that the so-called problems
of education, especially those relative to individuality, character and intellectual development,
have as their origin the permanent conflict between the child and the adult. The obstacles that
the adult places in the way of the child are
numerous and grave, and the degree of their
danger is dependent upon the consistency with
which the adult resorts to them—armed against
the child, as it were, with moral law, science and
the will to direct him according to his own con-
victions. It is therefore the adult closest to the
child, the mother or the teacher, who presents the
greatest danger to the formation of the child's
personality. This question of the primitive conflict between the strong and the weak is not only
relevant to education, but is reflected in the psychic life of the mature adult, providing the key to
much that is psychopathic and anomalous in his
character and emotions. The question takes on,
therefore, universal proportions of a cyclical na-

ture in that the problem passes from adult to child and from child to adult.

The first step in the integral resolution of the problem of education must not, therefore, be taken toward the child, but toward the adult educator: he must clarify his understanding and divest himself of many preconceptions; finally, he must change his moral attitudes. Another step follows this one: we must prepare an environment adapted to the child's life, one that is free of obstacles. The environment must be designed in terms of the needs of the child himself, who step by step will be freed from the necessity to combat obstacles and begin to manifest his own superior characteristics—those higher, purer tendencies of a new personality. These two steps are necessary to prepare a foundation for a new moral order for the adult as well as the child. In fact, having prepared an environment scaled to the child and having been exposed to the freedom created by his impulses toward activity, we have seen characteristics in the child who is tranquilly at work that have never been seen before. The environment adapted to the most elementary needs of the child's spiritual life revealed attitudes that had been hidden in the child; because of his lifelong conflict with the adult, he had been able to develop only defensive and repressive attitudes.

There exist, therefore, two psychic states in

the child: one that is natural and creative, therefore normal and superior, and one that is forced and inferior and that results from the battle in which the weak are attacked by the strong. A new image of the child has emerged from this discovery, which has been a beam of light to guide us on the road to a new education. The child demonstrates, along with his innocence, courage and faith in himself and is endowed with a moral force that also has a social direction. At the same time, those defects that one struggled in vain to discourage with education—that is, misbehavior, destructiveness, lying, shyness, fear and, in general, all those that are contingent upon the posture of defense—have disappeared. The adult who is in communication with this new child, that is, the teacher, has a whole new orientation: he is no longer the powerful adult but the adult made humble, serving the new life. Understanding the child's two psychological states, it is impossible to discuss education without first establishing the basis for the discussion: we must speak of the child under the powerful adult—when he is in a permanently defensive state, if he has not already been completely repressed—or we must speak of the liberated child whose condition of life is normal and who is permitted to manifest his creative capacities.

In the first case, the adult himself is the unknowing cause of the difficulties against which

he battles, lost in a forest of insoluble problems.
In the second case, the adult is conscious of his
errors and stands in a just relationship to the
child. In this case, the adult finds his way easy
and bright, a pacific new world full of marvels.

It is possible to practice the science of education within this second framework. Indeed, the
concept of science presupposes that a truth has
been discovered, that there is a secure basis for
progress, a sure and determinative method of
procedure and control against error. The guide
who provides such precision is the child himself;
he asks the adult who serves him to be helpful:
"Help me to help myself."

It is true that the child develops in his
environment through activity itself, but he needs
material means, guidance and an indispensable
understanding. It is the adult who provides these
necessities crucial to his development. The adult
must give and do what is necessary for the child
to act for himself; if he does less than is necessary, the child cannot act meaningfully, and if he
does more than is necessary, he imposes himself
upon the child, extinguishing his creative impulses. One can determine the limit, or what we
call the "threshold of intervention." This deter-
mination becomes more precise as, step by step,
we accumulate experience with our guide. The
necessary understanding between the adult edu-

cator and the child clarifies itself ever more exactly.

The child's activity arises in relationship to material things, that is, to objects scientifically selected and put at his disposal in his environment. In this lies the resolution of the problem of the acquisition of culture. It consists not only in limiting the intervention of the adult but also in shoring up the more traditional forms of teaching with materials that permit the child to acquire by himself the necessary understanding according to his own developmental needs. Every child who has achieved the liberty that arises out of activity develops according to the most profound, creative needs and progresses in the learning process; thus the development of individuality becomes an exercise conducive to the acquisition of culture. The teacher remains in her capacity as director and guide, but only when necessary; the child's personality arises according to its own laws, exercising its abilities to act.

We have derived many useful insights from actual experience, which have helped us to construct new guidelines for a scientific pedagogy of crystal clarity. One such guideline is that not only the intervention of the adult but also the educational materials and in general the environment itself must be limited. It is possible to have too little or too much material, and either is

155

deleterious to the child's development: a lack can cause arrestation, and an excess can result in confusion and the dispersion of energies. To clarify this concept, it is necessary to produce some analogous facts already noted. In eating, for example, undernourishment produces malnutrition, but overeating has toxic effects and predisposes the body to innumerable ills. It is well known that overeating does not invigorate but rather weakens, yet at one time it was believed that eating large amounts of food was conducive to health. Having corrected this error, doctors were able to arrive at precise standards for the quality and quantity of food necessary for the maintenance of health; indeed, the nutritional sciences seek ever more accurate measures.

Those who believe today that materials are the key to individual education often think that it is better to provide great quantities of materials without any system and without limit. These theorists can be compared to those in the past who thought that by eating without limitation one could achieve the best state of health. The parallel works perfectly because it deals with the question of feeding, in one case the body, and in the other the mind. Now, too, our studies of the means to intellectual development, that is, of materials, have begun to reveal limits ever more exactly capable of producing a full development and the greatest spontaneous activity. It is, however, always the new figure of the child that comes forth to guide such determinations.

The new child reveals himself even in the first few months of life. It is clear that those of us who thought that the only utilizable psychological facts were those pertaining to the conscious mind and to linguistic expression must have thoroughly neglected the very young child. The conviction that nothing can be offered the infant except physical care has obscured facts of the greatest importance. But when the adult is prepared to perceive the child's psychic manifestations rather than suppress them, then he can see clearly that the child's inner life is much more intense and precocious than had ever been supposed. Indeed, it has been revealed with the greatest clarity that even the smallest child is able to establish rapport with his environment. This rapport precedes his motor development; he has a living spirit and therefore needs help and spiritual care even when there is no motor or linguistic development. Therefore, the child's nature is dualistic and reflects a functional contrast between his psychic life and his physical life, a phenomenon different from that in other animals, whose instincts animate their movements almost at birth. Man must construct by himself the great instrument by which the spirit can reveal itself and act, which leads us to think of the characteristic superiority of man, who

157

must animate with his own ego the very complicated apparatus of his physical movement that
must finally come to serve his own particular
individuality. Man must construct himself, and
in the end, possess himself and direct himself.
Thus we see that a child is in continual motion,
for he must develop the relationship between
action and spirit little by little. While the adult's
activity is motivated by thought, the child is
impelled to construct a unity between thought
and action. This is the key to personality in the
process of development.

Because of this, those who impede the
child's movements build obstacles in the way of
his construction of personality. Thought arises
independent of action, and action obeys the commands of another person; motion does not respond to the proper spirit. Because of this, the
character is fragile, and an interior disunity pre-
vails that weakens every act. This is an important fact for the future of mankind and ought to
be considered as a first principle in the education
of the family as well as in the school.

The child is much more spiritually elevated
than is usually supposed. He often suffers, not
from too much work, but from work that is
unworthy of him. The interest of the child is
toward an effort appropriate for his great intellectual powers and the dignity of his person.
Now in thousands of schools in every part of the

world, I have seen the new children doing things that no one would have believed possible. In fact, little children have demonstrated the capacity of working for long periods of time without tiring, of concentrating in a manner completely remote from the outside world, thus revealing the constructive process of their personalities. They have shown themselves as singularly precocious in the question of culture: children of four-and-a-half have learned to write and have written with an enthusiasm and joy so great that we have defined it as an *explosion of writing*.

All such instruction is achieved with ease and enthusiasm and at a very early age, without exhaustion because it is spontaneous activity.

Observing these children—healthy, tranquil, innocent, sensitive, full of love and joy, always ready to help others—I have been forced to reflect upon the amount of human energy wasted because of an ancient error and great sin that disseminated injustice to the very roots of mankind. It is the adult who produces in the child his incapacities, his confusion, his rebellion; it is the adult who shatters the character of the child and deprives it of its vital impulses. And more than that, it is the adult who affects to correct the errors, the psychological deviations, the lapses of character that he himself has produced in the child. So we find ourselves in a labyrinth without an exit, in the presence of a

159

failure without hope. Until the adults consciously face their errors and correct them, they will find themselves in a forest of insoluble problems. And children, becoming in their turn adults, will be victims of the same error, which they will transmit from generation to generation.